STUDIES IN ENGLISH LITERATURES

Edited by Koray Melikoğlu

Lance Weldy

Seeking a Felicitous Space on the Frontier

The Progression of the Modern American Woman in O. E. Rölvaag, Laura Ingalls Wilder, and Willa Cather

STUDIES IN ENGLISH LITERATURES

Edited by Koray Melikoğlu

ISSN 1614-4651

4 *Paul Fox and Koray Melikoğlu (eds.)*
Formal Investigations
Aesthetic Style in Late-Victorian and Edwardian Detective Fiction
ISBN 978-3-89821-593-0

5 *David Ellis*
Writing Home
Black Writing in Britain Since the War
ISBN 978-3-89821-591-6

6 *Wei H. Kao*
The Formation of an Irish Literary Canon in the Mid-Twentieth Century
ISBN 978-3-89821-545-9

7 *Bianca Del Villano*
Ghostly Alterities
Spectrality and Contemporary Literatures in English
2nd, revised editon
ISBN 978-3-89821-714-9

8 *Melanie Ann Hanson*
Decapitation and Disgorgement
The Female Body's Text in Early Modern English Drama and Poetry
ISBN 978-3-89821-605-5

9 *Shafquat Towheed (ed.)*
New Readings in the Literature of British India, c.1780-1947
ISBN 978-3-89821-673-9

10 *Paola Baseotto*
"Disdeining life, desiring leaue to die"
Spenser and the Psychology of Despair
ISBN 978-3-89821-567-1

11 *Annie Gagiano*
Dealing with Evils
Essays on Writing from Africa
ISBN 978-3-89821-867-2

12 *Thomas F. Halloran*
James Joyce: Developing Irish Identity
A Study of the Development of Postcolonial Irish Identity in the Novels of James Joyce
ISBN 978-3-89821-571-8

13 *Pablo Armellino*
Ob-scene Spaces in Australian Narrative
An Account of the Socio-topographic Construction of Space in Australian Literature
ISBN 978-3-89821-873-3

Lance Weldy

SEEKING A FELICITOUS SPACE ON THE FRONTIER

The Progression of the Modern American Woman in O. E. Rölvaag, Laura Ingalls Wilder, and Willa Cather

ibidem-Verlag
Stuttgart

Bibliografische Information der Deutschen Nationalbibliothek
Die Deutsche Nationalbibliothek verzeichnet diese Publikation in der Deutschen Nationalbibliografie; detaillierte bibliografische Daten sind im Internet über http://dnb.d-nb.de abrufbar.

Bibliographic information published by the Deutsche Nationalbibliothek
Die Deutsche Nationalbibliothek lists this publication in the Deutsche Nationalbibliografie; detailed bibliographic data are available in the Internet at http://dnb.d-nb.de.

Cover illustration: *The Chrisman Sisters on a claim in Goheen settlement on Lieban (Lillian) Creek, Custer County, Nebraska, ca. 1886. © Nebraska State Historical Society.*

∞

Gedruckt auf alterungsbeständigem, säurefreien Papier
Printed on acid-free paper

ISSN: 1614-4651

ISBN-10: 3-89821-535-0
ISBN-13: 978-3-89821-535-0

Printed in Germany

Table of Contents

Foreword

The bulk of this study is a close reading of O. E. Rölvaag's *Giants in the Earth* (trans. 1927), Laura Ingalls Wilder's *Little House on the Prairie* (1935), and Willa Cather's *My Ántonia* (1918) from a feminist point of view with a definite inquiry into the concept of space. Marilyn R. Chandler rightly notes that "Space is an ideologically weighted 'product,' and the idea of space is a highly charged issue for theorists and artists" (3). It is important to highlight this point early on in this study for at least two reasons. First, this connection between space and ideology denotes a politically liminal place wherein questions of identity, in this study specifically with gender, complicate and influence the socio-cultural hierarchy. By referring to space as a "product," Chandler implies that this entity becomes ideological as a result of a dominant, active agent that relegates behavior, both subtly and overtly. Second, as the latter half of Chandler's sentence suggests, scholars and authors have scrutinized the politics of space through essays and novels: writers of fiction which could include Rölvaag, Wilder, and Cather, and scholars of spatial and feminist criticism such as Bachelard, Showalter, and Irigaray. As Elaine Showalter states, "feminist criticism has shown that women readers and critics bring different perceptions and expectations to their literary experiences, [indicating] that women have also told the important stories of our culture" (introduction 3). An obvious question here is, as Rowena Fowler asks, "Should men practice feminist criticism?" (51). I believe this is a legitimate question requiring more than a single-sentence response. In the following explanation, I focus first on feminism itself and then discuss where men fit into feminist criticism.

According to Victoria Walker, "There is no single, comprehensive definition of feminism; feminism knows neither 'founding mothers' [. . .] nor a distinctive methodology. At best, we may speak of feminisms" which "have touched upon a vast array of critical problems," such as "the reconstruction of women's history and of a female literary tradition" ("Feminist Criticism, Anglo-American"). For the purposes of my study, I will be incoroporating Anglo-American feminist critique. Before moving on to the specific focus of feminism, I want to stop here and recognize two points. First, the essence of feminism's multivalence does not preclude, but actually *invites* participation from diverse viewpoints, including perspectives from unlikely candidates such as men. Second, this lack of an established definition inhibits a gatekeeper, elitist mentality. Walker points to the purpose that Anglo-American feminist studies has in common with the rest of feminist criticisms: "that of exposing the mechanisms upon which patriarchal society rests and by which it is maintained, with the ultimate aim of transforming social relations." She goes on to say that this goal of transformation is common among all feminists because "they believe patriarchal society operates to the advantage of men and serves men's interests above all others." What we can surmise from Walker's conciseness is that, essentially, feminism considers mainstream society as "man-based" and desires to provide sexual equality.

Again, the question arises: "What place does a man have pointing out patriarchal insensibilities?" Fowler summarizes some of the scholarly controversy about men entering the feminist criticism conversation, noting that, while teaching women's texts to women students, it could be problematic for men to (consciously or unconsciously) elect themselves as the authority figure in the classroom, leaving little room for input from the women. She also says that "There is also a tendency for male feminists to absorb women's insights and research findings without properly acknowledging them [. . .]. The problem has been that the terms on which men are to join the debate are not clear" (52). In other words, men who venture into feminist criticism are not always sure if they have a legitimate voice, yet at the end of this passage Fowler suggests that breaking down gender barriers has been a positive byproduct of feminist criticism: "one of the most enviable achievements of feminist criticism has been to mix and merge or bypass the tired binary symbologies of male head and female heart" (55).

She concludes: "The debate must be carried on not between men and about women, not among women only, but between and among women and men as peers" (60). Elaine Showalter concurs: "This enterprise should not be confined to women; I invite [male critics] to share it with us" ("Towards" 142).

Though Fowler contests K. K. Ruthven's description of only extreme sides of feminist criticism, she would agree with him that men can engage in feminist discourse. According to Ruthven,

> It is no more necessary to be a woman in order to analyse feminist criticism as criticism than it is to be a Marxist in order to comprehend the strategies of Marxist criticism. In any case, whether or not men are eligible to take part in feminist literary studies at any level is an argument created and sustained solely within the domain of feminist discourse. It is not a problem which antecedes the invention of feminist criticism, but on the contrary is a function of it, and cannot possibly be regarded therefore as a prediscursive or extradiscursive mandate for the production of feminist criticism. This is as good a reason as any why men should not be put off by the intimidatory rhetoric of radical feminism, but confront the challenge of the new knowledge it proclaims by becoming involved not only in the production but also in the assessment of feminist criticism. (272)

Setting aside his statements on radical feminism, I found myself encouraged not only by Ruthven's comments, but also by women scholars like Fowler and Showalter who, in the words of Ruthven, discredit "essentialistic theories of human behaviour which designate certain characteristics as male-specific and others as female-specific" (264), thereby discrediting the notion that feminist scholars writing about women's issues must be female. I believe that William Handley has succinctly summarized the theoretical and scholarly direction for which I aim when he says, "I share in the revisionist spirit of feminist scholars who have moved the focus away from masculine genres to literature by women, yet I have chosen to focus on both genders in relation to each other—to see women and men in texts by women and men" (3). In this same vein, I supply, through each main chapter, footnotes that comment on men who have written about literary women in positions or mindsets similar to the discussed female protagonist of each chapter. In so doing, I show that authors of both genders have written about women in similar positions. It is with the help of these scholars and through the submission of these footnotes that I find my legitimacy when participating in feminist discourse.

1. Constructing a Felicitous Space: Theories of Space and Gender and Historical Backgrounds

Paula E. Geyh notes, "Space is not inert, a mere site or setting for the action of our lives and narratives, nor do subjectivities simply 'inhabit' spaces that exist independently of them" (103). Rather,

> Subjectivity and space are mutually constructing: while subjects constitute themselves through the creation of spaces, these same spaces also elicit and structure subjectivities. To understand postmodern subjectivities and space, we must explore the complex ways in which they construct one another. (104)

In other words, the space an individual occupies indicates and even helps to determine the kind of person that individual is. In her essay, Geyh focuses "on the ways in which feminine subjectivity both constitutes itself and is constituted either through or in opposition to the space of the 'house' or the 'home' [. . .]" (104).

It follows, then, that if space allocation is differentiated by gender, space and gender have a significant influence on each other—an influence that can vary with time and culture. Doreen Massey comments on this influence in *Space, Place, and Gender*, when she notices

> the intricacy and profundity of the connection of space and place with gender and the construction of gender relations. Some of this connection works through the actual construction of, on the one hand, real-world geographies and, on the other, the cultural specificity of definitions of gender. Geography matters to the construction of gender, and the fact of geographical variation in gender relations, for instance, is a significant element in the production and reproduction of both imaginative geographies and uneven development. (2)

Though Massey's project focuses on geography, gender, and space in the modern day work place, I think her concepts about geography can apply to the nineteenth century, where indeed geography affected gender, evidenced by women on the American frontier.

Indeed, in the past, women have been stereotypically assigned to the house, to the inside space. During Geyh's discussion, she pays careful attention to the windows of the house, which, she believes, indicate "the boundaries of the house," so that "the very structure of the house, which relies on those boundaries, is simultaneously engendered and endangered. The window's double nature is apparent in the way that, closed or open, it might either divide or connect the inside and the outside" (110-11). In American literature, the sharpest division between inside and outside spaces for women occurs on the frontier, especially on the prairie frontier.[1]

How do people respond to the land of the outside spaces? Or, better yet, how does the land respond to people? D. H. Lawrence believes that even to the frontiersman and immigrant in America, "the very landscape, in its very beauty, seems a bit devilish and grinning, opposed to us" (50). In the first place, then, open space on the American

[1] Renée Hirschon has made some interesting assertions about open and closed spaces in the context of discussing the role of woman in Greek society: "Among the conceptual categories of the society is a set of perceptions surrounding two opposed states: that of the 'open' and that of the 'closed'" ("Open" 76). Essentially, she says that "'opening' is an auspicious state; it is propitious and desired. 'Closing' is associated with misfortune, it is unfavorable and, in its ideal sense, should be avoided" (76). She goes on to discuss the various ways in which "closed" and "open" states occur in women's lives: "For the woman this auspicious state can only be achieved through conjunction with her husband [. . .]. His role as a medium of opening for the woman is not only a physical one, but exists too in the context of sociable exchange beyond the family" (78). Also, "The woman's use of space is defined and restricted in terms of the domestic imperative" (81). Hirschon also has another interesting article focusing on inside and outside space:

> In the wider context of social life the fundamental dichotomy of the 'house' and the 'road,' the inner and outer realms, is the point of orientation for interaction between women in the neighbourhood. This spatial and symbolic division is mediated, however, by two items—the kitchen, which is the diacritical marker of each conjugal household and the exclusive area of each married woman, and the movable chair. ("Essential" 72-73)

landscape—including the frontier—can be intimidating to at least some men. Second, if the landscape is naturally adverse to men, how much more harsh might the landscape be to women? Glenda Riley writes about this issue of women's adaptability to the frontier: "The prairie frontier, then, was not a particularly hospitable one for women. Given the nineteenth-century role expectations that, on the whole, women's lives would be domestically oriented, women were often disappointed with the setting and the resources that were offered to them by the prairie" (46). Both historians and novelists acknowledge that women experienced a rough time on the American frontier in the mid- to late nineteenth century. Few scholars agree, however, on the reasons for women's struggles on the frontier or on the ways in which women's relationships to frontier space changed over time. My purpose in this study is to focus on O. E. Rölvaag's *Giants in the Earth*, Laura Ingalls Wilder's *Little House on the Prairie*, and Willa Cather's *My Ántonia* to show how the female characters in these novels react to space and how space prevents or provides tranquility and growth for these frontier women. In so doing, I will show how these texts, each of which can be interpreted through a feminist lens, reveal feminine spatiality and gender struggles in the context of American culture and literary theory.

My desire to look at feminine spatiality stems from two major works. Gaston Bachelard's seminal work, *Poetics of Space,* served as the first spark for me. Although the bulk of Bachelard's book focuses on philosophical and phenomenological aspects of poetry and poetic images, the ninth section deals with poetic images central to this study—with images of closed and open spaces, specifically with a discussion of the space of the house. Fortunately, Bachelard's analysis of these images and of the significant concept that he calls "felicitous space" has also inspired other scholars. Diana Fuss' intriguing book, *The Sense of an Interior*, looks at the interior rooms of four great writers. She notes, "My own view on the relation between literature and architecture is one part Martin Heidegger, one part Gaston Bachelard.

[. . .] Bachelard in *The Poetics of Space* asserts that a building is a special kind of poetry" (4). The title of Judith Fryer's book, *Felicitous Space,* comes directly from the following introductory statement by Bachelard:

> In the present volume, my field of examination has the advantage of being well circumscribed. Indeed, the images I want to examine are the quite simple images of felicitous space. In this orientation, these investigations would deserve to be called topophilia. They seek to determine the human value of the sorts of space that may be grasped, that may be defended against adverse forces, the space we love. (xxxv)

Based on Bachelard's and Fryer's uses of the term, then, felicitous spaces are defined for the purposes of this study as "spaces of comfort, spaces people are familiar with, spaces without internal hostility."

One of the most captivating concepts that Bachelard discusses is how "the dialectics of large and small [offer a kind of] poetics of space" (xxxviii). By proposing various dialectics—between large and small, within and without, closed and open—Bachelard has provided a paradigm for scholars, including Fryer and the present researcher, to use in viewing literary texts. Fryer's *Felicitous Space* focuses specifically on works by Edith Wharton and Willa Cather. Her overriding critical question is "what *is* the relationship, in America, of space to the female imagination?" (49). One of her own answers is that the woman "has been denied, in our culture, the dialectical movement between private spaces and open spaces" (50). Though Fryer devotes considerable space to *My Ántonia*, her discussion focuses more on Jim's imagination than on the dialectic itself, which is the concept that I explore in my study of selected novels by Rölvaag, Wilder, and Cather. Nevertheless, Fryer's critical study serves as a model of how Bachelard's concepts can be applied to literature from a feminist perspective.

Concepts of Space and Gender on the American Frontier

Shirley Ardener says, "*space reflects social organisation*, but of course, once space has been bounded and shaped it is no longer merely a neutral background: it exerts its own influence" (12). As Ardener rightly notes, space turns into a social construct, and that social construct becomes the crux of my study because of the traditional power structure that has extended from the urban to the rural frontier of the United States, a power structure that awards open spaces to men. Space as a social construct serves as a relevant theme in my study, and I will often refer to feminist scholars like Diana Fuss who address this issue. She says that her book, *Essentially Speaking: Feminism, Nature & Difference*, "can be described as an investigation of the place of essence in contemporary critical discourse, but perhaps we should be interrogating not only the place of essentialism but the essentialism of place" (29). In other words, whereas scholars have well documented the phenomenon of how certain people have been stereotypically assigned different qualities, the identity politics involved with certain spaces is still a rather new topic to explore. In *Feminist Theory and Literary Practice*, Deborah L. Madsen spends a chapter on eco-feminism and its application to Willa Cather. In this chapter, she summarizes a few eco-feminist principles from scholars such as Ynestra King, who argues that the "relationship between men and women is the paradigm for oppressive hierarchical relationships: that which is dominant is gendered as masculine, that which is subordinate is feminised" (122). It follows from this paradigm, in conjunction with the works by scholars like Fuss, that spatial assignment can be and has been predicated by gender. Madsen points out that one of the ways to counterbalance this hierarchy is to dissolve the either-or binary.

When the geography of the frontier limits the amount of intimate, feminine space because of the rural setting and remoteness of neighbors, the social configuration invites disaster for pioneer women.

As Glenda Riley remarks, "frontierswomen's responsibilities, life styles, and sensibilities were shaped more by gender considerations than by region" (2). Drawing on Ardener's and Riley's assertions as well as the observations of Geyh previously discussed, I assign open space primarily to the masculine gender and closed space to the feminine. In general, closed space refers to women in the home, while open space concerns men working outside the home, be that in the fields, around the house, or on open ranges or places farther away.

Just as "[f]eminist scholarship rejects the idea of a literature produced in a social and historical vacuum" (Fowler 54), so too must a true feminist analysis of space in *Giants in the Earth*, *Little House on the Prairie*, and *My Ántonia* consider the historical and social context. In other words, the woman's perspective includes actions and events surrounding her, in this case, the historical westward movement. The role of the pioneer woman essentially required her to remain in closed spaces. As Susan H. Armitage explains, "The pioneer woman's major role was that of domestic provider and sustainer. She was responsible for feeding and clothing her children and her husband" (9). Women fulfilled this space as provider and sustainer by spending the majority of their time inside the home. Dean L. May provides an interesting historical account about pioneer families scattered around the western frontier. His focus on women in frontier communities in the 1860s promotes the idea that space has the power to give or delimit power for women. For the pioneer women in Sublimity, Oregon, "virtually everything produced on the farm involved the woman in an important role at some point in the process." This gave the women

> considerable influence *within* the home—for this folk the social world of most meaning to most persons of both sexes. Yet, when they moved beyond the family and close neighbor/kin group, their influence quickly diminished. More than a third of those over eighteen in Sublimity in 1860 could not read or write (35 of 94; the corresponding figure for men

> was 15 of 151, or 10 percent). Such women no doubt felt disadvantaged in situations requiring them to deal with those outside their neighbor/kin group. (May 135)

According to Glenda Riley, nineteenth-century pioneer women focused on their homes and families, while the men concentrated on making a living for those families (42). These traditional sex roles initially resulted in women working in inside spaces and men laboring outside.

During the nineteenth century, however, stereotypical spatial assignments for women migrating to the American West began a long but significant process of transformation. Julie Roy Jeffrey notes that "It was not until the [eighteen] seventies that pioneers pushed eagerly out onto the prairies of Minnesota, the Dakotas, Nebraska, and Kansas" (27), and oftentimes wives and mothers would accompany the men. In the environment of wagons, sod houses, and claim shanties, inside and outside spaces often became difficult to distinguish. Similarly, as Jeffrey argues, this same issue of gender role delineation was not always clear cut. And even though, as Jeffrey claims, this was the time for women to take advantage of new opportunities available to them, the majority did not capitalize on this. Their inability to do so stemmed from their uneasiness at embracing a whole new mindset, "even when forced into new ways of behaving. Possibly the polarization of sex roles which cast women into the role of the dependent, if superior, sex made it psychologically difficult to create sexual alternatives even when the environment seemed favorable" (Jeffrey 26). In other words, these women were leaving "civilization" and all the stereotypical gender roles that society entails, yet even on the prairie, where they had to learn to live in the masculine open spaces, they often found it difficult to assume a different kind of role in the family. Essentially, most pioneer women found themselves still clinging to their feminine roles.

Overview of the Study

Finally, I want to provide an overview of the three female characters who will serve as the main subjects of my study: Beret in *Giants in the Earth*, Laura in *Little House on the Prairie*, and the eponymous character in *My Ántonia.* In this section I will make relevant, but brief, connections between historical frontier experiences and the spaces experienced by each fictional character. In organizing my chapters, I begin by discussing Beret, move to Laura, and conclude with Ántonia because I believe this order best illustrates the gradual progression of women's spatial liberation on the frontier. I feel I ought to mention that this study is by no means comprehensive or representative of all cultures.[2] As Handley says, "My hope is that my readings will provide a way of thinking through such issues in other texts as well as the comparative functions of nostalgic retrospection; that it will offer a way of contrasting relations between the personal and the public" (8). For this study, the personal and public, inside and outside, and subject and object all dynamically interact and influence each other, and I want this study to serve as a catalyst for future research not only in Anglo-American cultures, but other diverse ones as well.[3]

---

[2] One example of a corroborating reaction to space from another culture can be found in the novel, *The Endless Steppe*, by Esther Hautzig. While teaching this book in a graduate summer seminar on multicultural adolescent literature, I was fascinated to see how Esther responded to her family's displacement from Poland to Siberia during the Jewish displacement of WW II. Her reaction to open spaces for the majority of the book corresponds to the phases of response by Laura Ingalls in *Little House on the Prairie.* Esther remarks that "Siberia was the end of the world, a point of no return" (42) and then interprets the land as a living, menacing entity: "Outside, the steppe was vast and silent—not even a bird was overhead that morning—and it became Popravka's accomplice in reducing us to insects" (52). Comments about her family's frontier spirit and Esther's gradual love for outside spaces can be found in the passages on pages 81, 94, 112, 113, 228, 236, and 239, respectively. Clearly, this topic of felicitous space is ripe for research, spanning multiple genres.

[3] One could look at diversity through race as well as genre. For example, Joyce Carol Thomas' picture book of poetry, *I Have Heard of a Land*, recounts a single, African-American mother's endeavor to establish her household on the open Oklahoma prairie during the time of the 1889 and 1893 Land Runs. The female protagonist is the obvious family leader who works outside as well as inside, as is illuminated by

In developing my analysis, I build on the criticism of other scholars. For example, Sylvia Grider discusses how Beret Hansa "cannot adjust to the emptiness and hostility of this new environment" (113); Carolyn Heilbrun's study of daughters' relationships to their parents finds that many daughters without brothers—a position held by Laura Ingalls—try to fill a son's role in the family, emulating the father rather than the mother (50); and a feminist perspective shows Ántonia Shimerda as finding "the challenge of maintaining domestic order against the disordered life of the frontier" (Fryer 247). In my study, I also incorporate the work of other feminist scholars like Nina Baym, who notices the gender-divided perspective of the landscape in which "[male] heroes of American myth turn to nature as sweetheart and nurture, anticipating the satisfaction of all desires through her and including among these the desires for mastery and power" (75), whereas a woman "is more likely to write of it [nature/landscape] as more active, to stress its destruction or violation" (75-76).[4]

Chapter 2 focuses on Beret, who succumbs to the vast open spaces and never finds a felicitous space. Many historians have documented the unhappiness and isolation felt by pioneer women like Beret. These women suffered infelicity for various reasons, including homesickness and the inability to cope with the startling environment. Jeffrey's comments about the westward influences upon women lends itself to my discussion of Beret's infelicity here, because she calls attention to

---

the text when it says that in this new land, a woman can "plant her crop and / walk all day and never come to the end of it" (5).

[4] It is important to note here two seminal works about frontier land coming from slightly different theoretical fields. First, Baym is probably referring to Henry Nash Smith's *Virgin Land*, which "traces the impact of the West, the vacant continent beyond the frontier, on the consciousness of Americans and follows the principal consequences of this impact in literature and social thought down to [Frederick Jackson] Turner's formulation of it" (4). Also, from a feminist point of view, Annette Kolodny's *The Lay of the Land* serves as a related source for Baym's discussion about landscape and gender. Kolodny argues, "From accounts of the earliest explorers onward, then, a uniquely American pastoral vocabulary began to show itself [. . .]. At its core lay a yearning to know and to respond to the landscape as feminine [. . .]" (8).

the issue of "contradictions" surrounding life in the house: "Women, unsullied by material interests, were supposed to find fulfillment at home. Yet, their ability to do so depended in some measure upon their husband's economic success" (32). Outside of "civilization," these women had to live without luxuries they were used to having. According to Henry Nash Smith, "the only value recognized by the theory of civilization is the refinement which is believed to increase steadily as one moves from primitive simplicity and coarseness toward the complexity and polish of urban life" (267). For the purpose of this discussion, "civilization" will refer to the elements inherent in urban life, whereas "uncivilized" suggests areas not yet structured for urban living. In the travel out West, women "coped with their sense of desolation by reproducing aspects of the world they left behind. Thus, women arranged their wagons, writing in their journals of the little conveniences they had fixed" (Jeffrey 38).

One of Beret's main ailments on the Dakota Territory is her melancholy, a melancholy that she feels no one else understands and that she cannot express to her family. She is deeply homesick for Norway, but as the caregiver, Beret knows she cannot encourage the family by sharing her depression. Jeffrey's discussion of how women coped with stress while traveling on the frontier adds to our understanding of Beret's predicament. According to Jeffrey, "The ways in which women handled their frustrations most often testifies [sic] to their attempts to live up to norms of female behavior, at least in front of their men" (48). Interestingly enough, "A fuller picture of the lives of Norwegian women on the prairies can be established than of any other group of ethnic women because of the relative abundance of Norwegian women's documents that are available" (Riley 31-32). Riley notes that journal entries written by Norwegian women living on the prairie express varied emotions. Because many of these women, like Beret, felt great helplessness and futility in the face of "uncivilized" open spaces, they may have developed defense mechanisms to the crude environment, pouring all of their energies into what they knew best—the domestic, inside sphere. These "transplanted" women "tried to recreate [their former "civilized" lives] on the prairie. [They] tried to reestablish what they thought of as civilization, not only in child rearing but also in every other aspect of their lives" (Riley 54). As chapter 2 shows, much of Beret's psychological trauma stems from her belief that their homestead is beyond the protective boundaries of the civilized world.

Readers familiar with Wilder's *Little House* series will find little trouble comparing Ma Ingalls to the previously mentioned Norwegian women who vie for a semblance of civilization on the open prairie. Ma, like Beret, considers herself in charge of maintaining cleanliness and an appearance of order around the house, and she assigns Laura and Mary some household chores as part of this maintenance. Like Beret, Laura Ingalls experiences some inconvenience and danger in traveling to the open frontier. However, Laura ultimately finds herself in a more positive position toward her new environment. Chapter 3 focuses on Laura Ingalls and how she negotiates her inner conflict between finding pleasure not only in interacting with Ma in the feminine space of the home, but also deriving equal personal fulfillment while working with Pa in the more masculine open areas. As a little girl on the prairie, Laura Ingalls crosses the "border spaces," as Susan Naramore Maher says (139), desiring the masculine open spaces and leaving the closed spaces to her ultra-feminine sister, Mary.

To reinforce the notion of gendered space in *Little House on the Prairie*, I include some observations about the lives of pioneering women, such as May's account of women in Sublimity:

> The tax lists of 1862 and 1871 record only two land parcels in women's names (in both instances widows), in spite of the Donation Land Act, which made it possible for wives to claim the same amount of land as their husbands and an 1866 Oregon law permitting women to own personal and real property in their own name. As noted, there are virtually no

> surviving accounts of formal women's activities outside the home until the 1880s. Apparently Sublimity's good wives rarely ventured beyond the kin/neighbor group that defined their social world. (135-36)

This report suggests the kind of behavior little girls like Laura saw in their frontier mothers. Even though women were allowed to "own" land in the outside space of the prairie, few early female pioneers took advantage of it. However, while migrant women in the American West might have been tentative in claiming outside space, their children—women of the next generation—found the transition much easier, as Laura's experience shows. Through a series of examples from Wilder's text—the construction of the house, the observation of the wolves through the window, and the digging of the well—this chapter will demonstrate how Laura navigates the gender border, arguing ultimately that, with Pa's encouragement, she favors the open, masculine spaces. Thus, Laura establishes herself as a literary example of a pioneer girl who embraces what women of Ma and Beret's generation cannot: the border between masculine and feminine space. However, even though Laura feels comfortable in masculine spaces, she does not permanently reside there, not completely in *Little House on the Prairie*, and even less so in subsequent books of the series, where she fully embraces her feminine space along with her physical maturity.

Chapter 4 shows how Ántonia Shimerda goes beyond Laura's border space to become a progressive, independent woman—successfully revolving between the two poles of an engendered-hybrid space. While Laura is comfortable in the border spaces, she cannot traverse completely into the male sphere for several reasons. Probably the most notable factor is her age, which prevents her from making her own decisions. On the other hand, Ántonia—also a pioneer girl from the younger generation—physically matures through the course of the novel and gradually integrates into masculine space. In his study, May recognizes women's gradual progression into the public, male sphere in communities like Alpine, Utah, where women "worked outside of the household in various community endeavors that took them early into public, male space" and where "women became in some senses more free. Many chores related to family production were no longer required. Their new role as consumers propelled them with greater frequency into male space and into new types of work, permitting in time a new sphere of independence" (May 143). After her father's death, Ántonia supports the family by working alongside her brother out in the fields, laboring in the open masculine spaces and gradually acquiring masculine physical attributes. With these masculine qualities come not only denigrating comments from traditional society, but also her independence. She is free to work where she wants to, whether that be out in the fields as a hired hand or in a home as a domestic laborer. As a possible explanation for such independence, Julie Roy Jeffrey submits that "emigration forced women to modify normal behavioral patterns" (25). As an emigrant from the Old World, Ántonia serves as an example of a literary woman faced with not only geographical differences on the frontier but also cultural differences in a new land. As such, she faces criticism from society whether she establishes herself in masculine or feminine spheres. This chapter, then, argues that Ántonia serves as an example of a pioneer woman who exists in both masculine and feminine spheres at certain times throughout the novel. Jeffrey goes on to say that "the frontier, which for most women began as soon as they left home and friends, challenged conventional sex roles and accepted modes of behavior" (25), a statement that definitely describes Ántonia's situation and gives larger meaning to the socio-historical context of my discussion of these three literary females.

Chapter 5 synthesizes my argument about the pioneer woman's evolving and dynamic reaction to felicitous space and the open spaces of the western frontier. By discussing the literary characters in the order of my chapters, I reiterate the sociological progression of the pioneer woman, a woman who moves from completely loathing to totally embracing vast spaces. Carol Fairbanks and Sara Brooks Sundberg's comment illustrates the spectrum of the literary pioneer women: "Women's reactions to the prairie landscape were as mixed as their attitudes toward emigration" (43). Though the stereotypical (and more than likely predominant) feelings of many women about traveling and living in the open masculine spaces of the western frontier might have been negative, other women increasingly found positive aspects about the prairie. I admire the frankness of Rosi Braidotti's prose when she says, "I deliberately try to mix the theoretical with the poetic or lyrical mode. These shifts in my voice are a way of resisting the pull toward cut-and-dried, formal, ugly, academic language" (37). Although I know I fail to inject my research with shifts of poetry, I strive to keep my prose from impeding my message.

2. Beret's Madness in Open Space: Oppressive Dialectics and the Elusiveness of Felicitous Space in *Giants in the Earth*

How did pioneering women, women who were used to assigned roles inside the house, react to the exposure to the open space? As Sylvia Grider puts it, "Settling the Plains was regarded by many men as the ultimate in excitement and adventure, but for women the experience was generally much more of an ordeal" (112). These women found themselves in a difficult and un-romantic move West, domesticating the little space they could find (most often inside the wagon) on the trail in the vastness of the open prairie. The "dialectics of large and small" (Bachelard xxxiv) contributed to the tension felt by pioneer women, and this concept is a useful focus for beginning the discussion of Beret Hansa, the Norwegian pioneer heroine in *Giants in the Earth,* who travels westward and experiences a long and difficult battle with the forces of nature on the prairie.

Published in English in 1927, the novel details the accounts of a Norwegian immigrant community as they settle in the Dakota Territory in the early 1870s. The story specifically focuses on the family of Per Hansa and Beret and tracks their marital, economical, and spiritual challenges over the course of almost a decade. While most everyone in the community struggles with the new environment, Beret particularly languishes in the open spaces of the prairie and suffers from severe depression, longing to return to Norway.

It is because Rölvaag's work focuses so much on the relationship between space and mental health that it is significant to critically analyze this text in light of theorists who write about space. Bachelard argues that "in exterior space, the imagination benefited from the relativity of size, without the help of ideas and, as it were, quite naturally" (xxxiv). Conversely, how does the imagination and mental health fare in interior spaces, and how does this affect gender? Unfortunately, because he conducts a phenomenological study of the imagination, Bachelard does not address the connection between space and gender.

Therefore, because of this lack of connection, I will first lay the groundwork of Bachelard's theories of the dialectic of inside and outside alongside a feminist look at social construction of identity as subject/object. Both of these theories will help me look closely at Beret's failure to cope in masculine space and to show how Rölvaag clearly demonstrates the non-felicitous experience Beret feels on the open spaces of the Dakota prairie.

As Bachelard says, "Outside and inside form a dialectic of division" (211), a division relevant to the discussion of the woman's historical role on the prairie compared to the traditional role of the pioneer man. As mentioned earlier, women's traditional place was in the domestic sphere of the home, where they worked mainly inside. So when women were forced to follow their husbands West for whatever reason, many of them found themselves internally conflicted, divided, left unsure about how to function in a world where they must not only take charge of the inside spaces of the home, but also live in the midst of an isolated, masculine open space.

Essentially, these pioneering families lived lives of uncertainty, wandering from place to place to find proper lodging. In *Nomadic Subjects: Embodiment of Sexual Difference in Contemporary Feminist Theory*—before arguing about the feminist as a nomadic individual in terms of identity—Rosi Braidotti discusses two other possible modes of self: the exiled and the migrant. Her discussion of the migrant female identity describes Beret's condition as a migrant very well:

> The migrant [. . .] is caught in an in-between state whereby the narrative of the origin has the effect of destabilizing the present. This migrant literature is about a suspended, often impossible present; it is about missing, nostalgia, and blocked horizons. The past acts as a burden in migrant literature; it bears a fossilized definition of language that marks the lingering of the past into the present. (24)

Definitely, Beret finds herself dangling in time, dissatisfied with the present because she has no desire to settle in the Dakota Territory. She is nostalgic for Norway, where she feels her life had better meaning, even though in Norway Beret's life was filled with a battle between her love for her parents and her love for Per Hansa. Through the lens of Braidotti's migrant female identity, Beret's immigrant chest that she holds so dearly serves as a concrete objectification of her nostalgic longings. Through the psychological narration, she speaks/thinks in past perfect and wishes to be at home in the Old World. In the chapter, "The Heart That Dared Not Let in the Sun," we discover that "She had been gotten with child by him out of wedlock," yet her "parents, in fact, had set themselves against the marriage with all their might, even after the child, Ole, had come" (224). Her parents think ill of him, and all Beret can longingly think about is "those kind-hearted parents on whom she had turned her back in order that she might cleave to him" (224). She even recalls that her parents had offered to raise the child. Because she chose to marry, to move to America, and to move out West, her horizons have been blocked, both mentally and physically. As a migrant, her identity is in limbo, and she has no power to construct herself. As a woman, she recalls that her husband "had been life itself to her; without him there had been nothing. . . . Therefore she had given herself to him, although she had known it was a sin—had continued to give herself freely, in a spirit of abandoned joy" (224). Notice that words like "nothing" and "abandoned" further perpetuate Beret's migrant, wandering identity that seeks to find stability in something outside of herself.

The overall meaning we can take for the definition of "felicitous space" is one of safety and comfort. But throughout Rölvaag's story, Beret finds little of either quality. At the beginning of the story, the Hansa family has been separated from the other Norwegian families traveling from Minnesota for the same desired destination. Beret, driving the oxen, is frightened at the thought of being lost in the open space. Rölvaag describes their situation by saying that the whole family "might just as well have dropped down out of the sky" because "their course was always the same—straight toward the west, straight toward the sky line" (6). Traveling in the same direction with no change of scenery instills a tiring monotony that serves as a seed of delusion, delusion that will bloom in a horrible manner near the end of Rölvaag's story. That the family is lost in this monotony certainly does not help the situation. Beret, nervous after asking her son if he has seen any sign of the others, feels hopelessness creep in, and she remarks that their present course "'seems to be taking us to the end of the world . . . beyond the end of the world!'" (8). Essentially, Beret sees the end of the world as the largest open space possible, an open space that offers no solace for her. A few paragraphs later, Rölvaag writes that "[a]t the moment when the sun closed his eyes, the vastness of the plain seemed to rise up on every hand—and suddenly the landscape had grown desolate; something bleak and cold had come into the silence, filling it with terror" (9-10). Night changes the open prairie, and the "vastness" becomes a formidable presence, instilling the reader (and most certainly Beret) with an unsettling feeling. Beret's emotional condition in reaction to this uprising of the vast prairie becomes apparent as she discovers they must still travel into the evening hours: "She shifted the child over into the other arm and began to weep silently" (10).

As Judith Fryer notes, "Women mythologized neither the landscape nor the trip itself. They traveled through an unknown landscape, neither virginal nor maternal, noting in their diaries not natural formations but numbers of graves; their journeys meant death and separation, illness, hardship, every kind of privation" (246). Though Beret does not keep a diary of her troubles or witness death while on the trail, she meets a traveling woman who does encounter death on the trail. After Beret and her family are established on the prairie, they meet a traveling Norwegian family that seems to mirror the Hansa family in several ways. Like the Hansas, this family began their journey with several other families. As Jakob says, "'We were five, you see, to begin with—five in all—but the others had to go on'" (Rölvaag 318). Most notably, Rölvaag's descriptions of Kari, Jakob's wife, indicates to the reader a connection to Beret: "Inside sat a woman on a pile of clothes, with her back against a large immigrant chest; around her wrists and leading to the handles of the chest a strong rope was tied; her face was drawn and unnatural" (317). The connection/comparison between Kari and Beret is quite obvious, especially with the immigrant chest serving as the nostalgic object of commonality between them. Again, through Braidotti's lens, notice how Kari's example here demonstrates the ultimate nostalgia of female, migrant identity: a woman not only longs for the land of her childhood, but also for a time when her child was living. Her migrant, female identity is so strong here that she has to be tied down to the very physical object that Beret herself will find herself attached to in a very physically intimate way. This immigrant chest serves as the controlling metaphor of longing throughout this novel, controlling the minds and lives of both Kari and Beret. Several times Rölvaag has already mentioned Beret's fixation with her own immigrant chest, and an "unnatural" face combined with a woman bound by rope suggests that she, like Beret, is not quite normal in this setting. Furthermore, Rölvaag distinctly mentions the "bond of understanding" between the two women (317) before Jakob explains Kari's story, a story that supports Fryer's assertion: "'Physically she seems to be as well as ever—as far as I can see. She certainly hasn't overworked since we've been traveling. I hope there's nothing wrong with her. . . . But certain things are hard to bear—I suppose it's worse for the mother, too—[. . .]. You see, we had to leave our youngest boy out there on the prairie. . . ." (Rölvaag 319-20). The death of their boy Paul has caused Kari great hardship.[5]

[5] Joseph Kirkland's *Zury: The Meanest Man in Spring County* (1887) depicts another woman, Selina Prouder, who experiences the loss of a loved one on the frontier. As Robert Thacker notes, "Kirkland, less bleak but equally realistic, recreates for his readers Selina Prouder's golden first vision of their homestead, but follows this almost immediately with the death of her daughter" (133).

Bachelard's dialectic of the division of outside and inside is a perfect illustration of this matrix of gender and place. The dialectic of inside and outside plays an integral part in feminine space. Beret experiences not only confinement in her assigned, contracted space, but also contraction within a vastness. As Beret serves the meal that night, Rölvaag points out that on "the blanket stood two dishes of porridge—a large dish for the father and the two boys, a smaller one for the mother and And-Ongen [the daughter]" (12). In this instance, Beret and And-Ongen's dish represents the signified, smaller space women were assigned.

Echoing Braidotti's earlier concepts of a migrant sense of self, Beret's identity as a constricted, constructed object—constricted space within a vast space—becomes even more apparent that same night, when Per Hansa, who has gone to look for any signs of their friends whom they are following, comes back to his home camp to find Beret sitting on the wagon tongue. When asked why she was outside in the middle of the night, Beret responds, "'It felt so awful to lie there alone, after you had gone. . . . I could hardly breathe . . . so I got up'" (21). This instance shows how lost Beret feels in the open prairie's vastness and also how she feels physically isolated, so much so that psychologically her respiratory system fails her, causing her lungs to contract within her own constricted physical body, thus restricting her breathing capabilities. Beret's migrant sense of self here succumbs to what Braidotti calls the fear of "missing, nostalgia, and blocked horizons" (24), especially when Beret can't see past the openness of the frontier.

Not only is Beret's identity constructed as migrant, but it is also socially constructed as a physical object, specifically with the controlling metaphor of the immigrant chest. Luce Irigaray's first chapter in *An Ethics of Sexual Difference* lays down the construct for her theoretical discussion of this issue. She notes,

> If traditionally, and as a mother, woman represents *place* for man, such a limit means that she becomes *a thing*, with some possibility of change from one historical period to another. [. . .] The maternal-feminine remains the *place separated from 'its' own place*, deprived of 'its' place. She is or ceaselessly becomes the place of the other who cannot separate himself from it. Without her knowing or willing it, she is then threatening because of what she lacks: a 'proper' place. [. . .] Centuries will perhaps have been needed for man to interpret the meaning of his work(s): the endless construction of a number of substitutes for his prenatal home. From the depths of the earth to the highest skies? Again and again, taking from the feminine the tissue or texture of spatiality. In exchange—but it isn't a real one—he buys her a house, even shuts her up in it, places limits on her that are the opposite of the unlimited site in which he unwittingly situates her. He contains or envelops her with walls while enveloping himself and his things with her flesh. (10-11)

How apt this passage is for better understanding Beret! As I will discuss shortly, her spatiality has been shut inside the sod house that Per Hansa has built for her. Instead of this house serving as a gift of love, it connotes his ability to confine her. In an act of love, Per actually paints the inside walls white. Beret looks at the walls that Per had made and of which he "was especially proud" (198). This was a unique decoration in that community. Nevertheless, as Irigaray notes, the construction of the house and the elements of the house serve as a means of confinement. Beret has become an object to be placed inside a bigger object. The inside white-washed walls blind her at times, leaving her incapacitated. During the winter, "there was nothing but whiteness outside [. . .]. Her eyes were blinded wherever she looked, either outdoors or indoors [. . .] and so she always looked down now, as she sat in the house" (199). The very picture of her as blinded, looking down at the floor, gives an image of an objectified woman in a forlorn, dejected state. Likewise, as we later discover that Beret succumbed to premarital sex—an act she remembers with guilt throughout her stay in the Dakota Territory—we realize Beret's body has, in the words of Irigaray, been sexually enveloped by Per Hansa. Her role as a socially constructed object has been sealed even before she has married him. Beret is frightened in this open space, and her words remind us of Bachelard's questions: "Where can one flee, where find refuge? In what shelter can one take refuge? Space is nothing but a 'horrible outside-inside'" (218). Again, Bachelard's analysis of Henri Michaux's poem fits Beret's condition: "the mind has lost its geometrical homeland and the spirit is drifting" (218).

Keeping in mind Irigaray's discussion of constructing confinement, we can see how even the process of building the house brings terror to Beret. After the Hansa family reunites with the others, they set up a temporary house in the wagon before they can construct a sod house. As Per Hansa travels to Sioux Falls for "an application for the quarter-section of land which lay to the north of Hans Olsa's" (36), Beret spends the time arranging the new living quarters, and though she enjoys the work, she notices "something vague and intangible hovering in the air [that] would not allow her to be wholly at ease" (37). This intangible fear[6] becomes clearer later in this same passage as Beret remarks that the vast open space of the prairie provides "nothing even to hide behind!" (37). In effect, the masculine open space terrifies her. Moreover, as Rölvaag notes, the "infinitude surrounding her on every hand might not have been so oppressive [. . .] if it had not been for the deep silence" (37). To Beret, this silence equals deprivation of life, desolation, a veritable wasteland where a woman comfortable with her assigned closed spaces panics, equating the vastness with the disturbing stillness: "How could existence go on, she thought, desperately? If

[6] Beret's intangible fear here appears similar to A.B. Guthrie's *These Thousand Hills* (1956). According to Fred Erisman, "Lat Evans's wife, Joyce, finds in Montana 'space that was a fear with nameless fears inside her'" (165).

life is to thrive and endure, it must at least have something to hide behind!" (Rölvaag 38). As her children gather Indian stones, she ponders her life "on a little green hillock, surrounded by the open, endless prairie, far off in a spot from which no road led back" (40). It is with subtle terror that she realizes that no road will lead her back to civilization, away from the oppressive, open spaces where her family is settling.

Rölvaag's description of the open spaces merges into an anthropomorphism of masculine oppression, further objectifying Beret. That night on their way back to their camp, Beret believes the evening dusk "seemed to gather all its strength around her, to close in on every side, to have its centre in the spot where she stood" (41). Again, Beret feels an invisible contraction of space within the vast prairie, and again, her claustrophobia comes at night. This time, Beret feels the night is toying with her, pursuing her. She is so distraught that night that she cannot sleep and listens to the discomforting winds. Diana Fuss, in *The Sense of an Interior*, briefly discusses the theoretical and historical nature of anthropomorphism, saying that this concept really came to the forefront because of the spread of capitalism in the 1800s. She scrutinizes the polarity between the "material object" and the "human subject: "Critical terms like anthropomorphism and alienation signal philosophy's continued discomfort with the mystifications and estrangements that attend the historical conflation of subject and object, another binary yet to be adequately challenged in cultural criticism" (14-15). Rölvaag's ability to anthropomorphize nature in order to give a gloomy presence outside furthers Fuss' notion about the objectification of the human subject as well as the concurring sentiments by Braidotti and Iragaray. Beret has already been established as merely an object to keep after the house. Hansa has built the house as a confining object for Beret, and Beret's tendencies oftentimes focus on the immigrant chest—a nostalgic object. Furthermore, Rölvaag inserts passages like the one near the end of the "Home-founding" chapter to paint a sinister picture of the masculine space: "The Great Plain watched them breathlessly" (61). The fate of Per Hansa at the end of the book seems to reinforce the notion that nature, the outside space, is vindictive. Ironically, Beret turns into an object at the climax of her mental instability as she hides inside her Norwegian chest during the grasshopper storm. The controlling metaphor of Beret's nostalgic, female identity serves as Irigaray's envelope. In a sense, she has become a physical thing to be kept stored away by a material object.

Needless to say, Beret cannot celebrate with Per Hansa upon his return with the deed to the land; rather, she can only stand "smiling at him, with tears in her eyes, beside the improvised house that she had made" (42). The smile is forced, with ambiguous tears, tears that the reader realizes to be from sorrow and terror, while Per perhaps interprets them to be from joy. For Beret, her tears represent the nostalgia of a world she can never return to. As a woman struggling to find a sense of stability and comfort in closed space, Beret's "improvised" house represents the closest element of familiarity. Nevertheless, even this modified sense of stability cannot allay her fears. After first deciding not to share her feelings, she tells Per, "'I'm so afraid out here!' She snuggled up against him, as if trying to hide herself. 'It's all so big and open . . . so empty'" (43). Nan Johnson's *Gender and Rhetorical Space in American Life, 1866-1910*, elucidates Per Hansa's reply to Beret's sincere fears. Rölvaag writes, "Per Hansa laughed loud and long, so that she winced under the force and meaning of it. 'There'll soon be more people, girl . . . never you fear'" (43). Per Hansa's flippant response and rhetorical silencing of Beret resemble an excerpt that Johnson provides from Florence Hartley's book, *The Ladies Book of Etiquette and Manual of Politeness* (1882) that relates to how ladies should behave when in conversation with men. Johnson remarks,

> Hartley's advice to women not to ask questions of professional men not only makes the point that women have no need to know about the details of the male-dominated profes-

> sions, but also stresses a rhetorical profile of silence or accommodation. Women do not ask questions, and they do not assert their opinions. Hartley's encouragement to women that they strike a pose of accommodation in conversation reinforces an ideological link between gender and rhetorical behavior by constructing yet another version of the noble queen who rules quietly in the home blending the correct atmosphere of politeness with the wine of silence. (66)

Consider Beret's role in the house. She clearly is uncomfortable living there and tries to express this discomfort to Per Hansa. Johnson's discussion here about women and men's profession can be translated to women and men's "business" pertaining to the home. While Beret is in charge of life in the house to some extent, she cannot control family matters, such as the location of their lodging, etc. Furthermore, Beret's rhetorical space has been curtailed as much as her physical space. Her words mean nothing to him, and her rhetorical appeal to his pity (*ad misericordium*) has failed. Beret's desire to hide herself reinforces the connection that pioneer women have with closed space. Nevertheless, even an "improvised house" cannot neutralize the powerful open space of the Dakota prairie. Fryer says these pioneering women "found in the journey west the challenge of maintaining domestic order against the disordered life of the frontier" (247). For Beret, this struggle to maintain a semblance of civilization eventually drives her crazy.

Although, like Ántonia, Beret interacts with the open spaces, in particular with the land, she does not find any joy in the work. Before the sod house is constructed, Beret, who has recently discovered she is pregnant, finishes housework hurriedly for two days and "pitche[s] in beside them [the men] and take[s] her full term like any man" (50). Her capacity for men's work, even though she is pregnant, is sufficient for her to partake in some outdoor duties. She also helps Per Hansa plant potatoes. Yet she finds no satisfaction in her work as Ántonia does. This lack of joy stems from the fact that cultivating and working the land settles the family deeper into the vastness of the prairie (51), the open place where Beret feels most uncomfortable. In her nostalgic voice, she thinks to herself, "Perhaps in time I will learn to like it, too" (51), though we as readers highly doubt it.

Beret's psyche, fragile through the first chapters of settling in the place, cannot comprehend much of anything beyond her fear of the open space. Marliyn Chandler's book, *Dwelling in the Text: Houses in American Fiction*, analyzes the affect of houses on literary characters. She remarks, "American writers have generally portrayed the structures an individual inhabits as bearing a direct relationship to the structure of his or her psyche and inner life and as constituting a concrete manifestation of specific values" (10). This correlation between house and psyche is evident for Beret, especially with the white-washed walls of the inside of the sod house. The Hansa house is made of sod—earth—ground outside in the open spaces. Consequently, this same sod forms an inside space and induces the blindness and physical incapacity for Beret as she struggles with the overwhelming brightness in the house. The oppressive structure permeates into her constructed identity, leaving the structure of her psyche unstable. In other words, this incapacity reflects her mental instability.

A further example of just how traumatizing the open space is for Beret's nostalgic identity comes when Per Hansa suggests that Beret take the children to visit the neighbors while he is gone to retrieve timber, but Beret, always mindful of the terror of the open space, does not dare wander outside after dark. She can think of the prairie at night only as the "whole desolation of a vast continent [. . .] centring [. . .] and drawing a magic circle about their home" (57). To Beret, this magic is actually a curse, and her fear of the prairie consumes her thoughts, disallowing any reality of the situation. For example, when someone suggests Per Hansa's tardiness in returning home stems from his acquiring fuel for winter, Beret's preoccupation with her geographical situation blinds her, to her dismay, to the reality that their family will actually stay long enough to face the winter. That Beret will dwell in the Dakota Territory long enough to witness the seasons changing seems to suggest that this open space is "not only a carefully conceived and artistic device used by Rölvaag to delineate character and to provide a crucible for the pioneers of Spring Creek, but also an ever-present, ever-changing and native force in the lives of the pioneers" (Ruud 218). For Beret specifically, this "force" is anything but positive.

Beret's fear soon becomes apparent to Per Hansa, who realizes that everyone has a fear on the prairie and believes "the women were the worst off; Kjersti feared the Indians, Sörine the storms; and Beret, poor thing, feared both—and feared the very air" (65). It is not by coincidence that the women's fears pertain to elements involved with the open spaces of the prairie: one would normally directly encounter Indians and storms by being outside in the open space. And Beret's fear is the worst of all—"the very air." As crucial as it is to survive with "air," she cannot tolerate the open space nor find a felicitous element in it. But Beret's awareness of Kjersti's fear of Indians as Beret struggles with Per Hansa's heroism—saving the old Indian with blood poisoning—also causes significant trauma for her. Returning to Per Hansa in the night, at the zenith of her fear of the prairie, she sleeps with Per Hansa, but not without violent tears: "Her body shook with sobs; they tore her so convulsively that she could not speak a word. Like a crushed thing she sank inertly to the ground" (83). Rölvaag's choice of words supports Bachelard's dialectic here. Beret, a woman used to closed spaces, languishes in open space, and reacts to the situation in a form of utter concession, "crushed" into a contracted form, yielding to the ground, the open ground against which she is utterly opposed.

In light of Braidotti and Irigaray's theoretical input, it is important to see how the physical objects of the window and the immigrant chest factor into both Beret's objectification and spatiality confinement. Beret's suffering in the vast open space continues as Per Hansa finds other reasons to leave her alone for days on end. She expresses her discomfort at the thought of Per Hansa's leaving home to search for some missing cattle, the incident that begins Rölvaag's focus on Beret's obsession with windows as the medium between her familiar, closed space and the strange, open space of the prairie. The same window that helps her view the departure of her husband also serves as a source of fear because of its proximity to the vastness of the prairie. Because of this fear, Beret "hung some heavy clothes up over the windows—the thickest clothes she could find—to shut out the night" (107). As is evident in previous episodes, night on the prairie instills the greatest fear in Beret. It is notable that Beret pulls "the big chest in front of the door" (107) not only because this chest represents the nostalgic elements of her former life in Norway and serves as a barricade against the prairie of the New World, but also because of its importance as an object container later in the story. The immigrant chest itself represents security and stability from Beret's past, yet it also serves as an object to conceal and confine. Upon his return, Per Hansa gives Beret a birdcage with a rooster and two hens. His gift appropriately fits Beret's position; she too feels caged. However, since Beret seems somewhat comfortable in the home environment and closed space, her discomfort would not necessarily lie in being in a cage, but rather, being in a cage surrounded by the vastness of the open prairie.

Beret's feminine psyche becomes noticeably broken down month by month. By the fourth month in this establishment, Beret clearly realizes that her feminine space and psyche are threatened by the vastness of the prairie: "Beret had now formed the habit of constantly watching the prairie; out in the open, she would fix her eyes on one point of the sky line—and then, before she knew it, her gaze would have swung around the whole compass [. . .]. Life it held not; [. . .] How could human beings continue to live here while that magic ring encompassed them?" (126-27). Later Beret discusses the detriment of the vast open spaces: "People had never dwelt here, people would never come; never could they find home in this vast, wind-swept void"

(127). And a little later, she believes that the open sky, in all its vastness, threatens "to draw in and choke her" (127); thus she fears the ultimate constriction of death.

Even when more and more settlers visit the area, Beret finds herself struggling in her own solitude, lost in what she considers an "eternal, unbroken wilderness in every direction" (131). This eternal wilderness invades her psyche and drives her deeper into her own closed space, where she lives in her own inner stillness within the contracted space of the sod house. When Kjersti visits Beret, she sees that while the boys are running around the house, "Beret listened in a rigid, frozen silence" (150).

The effects of the adverse conditions for Beret lead to physical and psychological constriction. Upon confronting Per Hansa's manipulation of the stakes on their property, Beret finds herself "overcome by a sudden feeling of suffocation" (154), a suffocation which results from her socially constricted airwaves. Her anger drives her from the contracted space to the vastness of the outside, where in her utmost fear of the outside, in the "pitch dark" (155), Beret seeks some refuge from her constricted environment. It is not coincidental here that she again sinks to the earth, a sign of yielding to her adversary—the outside space.

By October, this dialectic between inside and outside leaves Beret apathetic. She seems to have resorted to a habitual knitting session by the window: "her gaze constantly wandered out-of-doors, flitting back and forth over the section of the plain that lay in her view" (156). She is consumed with viewing a masculine space that she cannot experience freely. In this same passage, Rölvaag notes that as she gazes into this vastness of space, she keeps her gaze on an indeterminate object as though she is in a trance. Store-Hans notices his mother's blank stare and asks a significant question: "'What do you want, Mother?'" (157). Though her gazing at the window could suggest that Beret desires the freedom to roam through the masculine open spaces, she instead finds herself an "exile in an unknown desert" (158).

Diana Fuss' comment on houses in *The Sense of an Interior* can be applied to Beret's reaction to her living conditions on the prairie: "What is new about dwelling in the nineteenth century is the sense of structural encasement, of material containment that, for the dweller, can be as disorienting as it is reassuring, as debilitating as it is intoxicating" (9). For Beret, the sod house has done nothing but "encase" her in disorientation and debilitation, especially with her mental grasp on reality. The Hansa family recognizes certain spaces as being relegated to the women, as evidenced by Per Hansa's leaving home for a whole week and leaving different duties to the different sons. This particular passage resembles the relegation of space and the binary of men/women and subject/object that Doreen Massey discusses: "Danger and drudgery; male solidarity and female oppression—this sums up a classic view of life in many colliery villages during much of the nineteenth century. Here the separation of men's and women's lives was virtually total: men were the breadwinners, women the domestic labourers" (193). Just as Ma Ingalls finds herself relegated to the inside space, so too does Beret toil inside.[7] To the oldest son, Ole, Per Hansa gives the outdoor chores of taking care of the cattle and the wood supply, while "Store-Hans should serve as handy man to mother indoors" (166). Store-Hans's reaction to this allotment illustrates not only the assigned space for a woman, but also the resentment of a male being assigned to that closed, feminine space: "The disappointment hit Store-Hans the harder; here he would have to go pottering around like a hired girl—just like another woman!" (166). The fact that "The father pitied him [Store-Hans] more than this older brother"

[7] Mary Ellen Snodgrass writes in the chapter, "Short Fiction of the Frontier," that Hamlin Garland's Mrs. Haskins in "Under the Lion's Paw" expresses this same concern of women and work: "One of the first of early-twentieth-century writers to acknowledge the crushing load on farm wives, Garland depicts Mrs. Haskins as a meager survivor on the brink of collapse, a mother and housewife whose chores spool endlessly into the future, long after her youth is spent, her marriage eclipsed by drudgery" (346).

also shows that these notions of assigned feminine space—and the inferiority implied with it—have passed from father to son.

The feminist dialectic becomes greatly weakened through the allocation of assigned space. Not only does Beret find the outside space constricting, but she also experiences constriction in inside space. Beret's inability to establish a felicitous space becomes even more apparent as she becomes more and more delusional within the contracted space of the sod house. Her sanity comes into question as Rölvaag describes how she misplaces ordinary objects, looks for these objects, forgets what she is doing, and then sits down with a "peculiarly vacant look on her face" (180), signifying the vacancy and openness of the frontier overwhelming the felicitousness of her closed, feminine body. Not only does Beret's mental health decline, but her physical strength also wears down within the enclosed, feminine space. Alone with the children when Per Hansa and the men leave for a few days, Beret handles the boys' rowdiness about the supposed bear sighting and the boys' "vile language" in an unorthodox manner. In one of the most comedic yet disturbing scenes involving Beret's behavior, her belated reaction to her sons' uncivilized behavior supports the feminist dialectic of a struggle with assigned space: "Going straight over to the table, she began to lay about her with the switch; she seemed beside herself, struck out blindly, hit whatever she happened to aim at, and kept it up without saying a word" (184). The situation is a disturbing reflection of one woman's desperate struggle against a terrifying vast space that forces her to remain in closed spaces. After an unpleasant badger-eating episode, Beret hangs "more clothes over the window than she had the evening before" (188). Her fear of the outside wilderness grows. The windows are a transparent object that serve as a medium to outside spaces, but also are an object to delimit mobility to get to those outside spaces.

The night Per Hansa returns, Beret experiences a temporary relief when she, realizing she hasn't covered the windows, chooses not to do so because it is "nonsense" (195). However, the next day, Beret again becomes consumed with the window and its adjacency to the vastness of the prairie; looking eastward toward Norway where she wants to return, she notices the ensuing darkness and covers the window that night (196). Her obsession with looking out the window by day and covering it by night continues. During the day she looks through the window for the men, ready to come home to eat; however, "[t]heir liveliness and loud laughter only drove her heavy thoughts into a still deeper darkness" (198), a vast darkness similar to the very vast darkness she dreads in the open prairie.

The window also brings about a temporary blindness for Beret. As mentioned previously, after Per Hansa has limed the inside walls of the sod house white, the snowfall outside enhances the brightness everywhere Beret looks, except for the floor, so "she always looked down now" (199). The image of a woman forced to look down because of an inability to see suggests that this woman is incapable of controlling anything—from vision to action—about her situation. The vast open space seeps into Beret's feminine closed space and renders her an invalid at the mercy of the masculine elements. Unable to find a felicitous space within the closed space, Beret turns into a madwoman:[8] "going about shabby and unkempt; she didn't even bother to wash herself" (209). And her ability to manage familiar objects within her territory deteriorates as Per Hansa notices Beret losing commonplace items, even though the items are in plain sight. Store-Hans's comment—"'It looks as if your eyes were in your way!'" (211)—reinforces Beret's inverse blindness (not only in processing outward stimuli, but also recognizing what's happening to her inward faculties) as well as her inability to control her own space.

---

[8] An obvious connection to this assertion of Beret's madness comes in *The Madwoman in the Attic*. Gilbert and Gubar's monumental feminist work is somewhat relevant to this discussion because it focuses on literary women and their subjection to space. However, Gilbert and Gubar's focus on literary women in British literature does not easily fit with my analysis of frontier pioneer women. Nevertheless, it seems that Beret transforms from angel to monster, the two extreme categories that Gilbert and Gubar claim literary patriarchs use for women.

Diane Price Herndl's book, *Invalid Women: Figuring Feminine Illness in American Fiction and Culture, 1840-1940*, gives a great understanding into the range of women's infirmities for this time period. She discusses three major interpretations of illness of women in the nineteenth century, and Beret's troubles seem to revolve between Herndl's first two listings: first, "the result of 'cultural conditioning,' patriarchal oppression, and the masculine power to define and control women's bodies" as well as, second, those "who speak of illness not as the result of oppression but as the resistance to it" (6). Beret's condition of mental instability could be seen as a result of her having to move to the middle of nowhere and suffer to live long periods of time in social isolation inside their sod house, while her husband actively interacts with the outside world. For a while, Beret's mental instability worsens, yet lightens minimally after her pregnancy with Peder Victorious. In a sense, Beret's mental instability could be seen as both initially a *result of* her oppression as well as a *resistance to* it later in the novel. As for identifying Beret's malady, Herndl brings up an interesting point about diagnosis and class structure, noting that in the latter part of the 1800s, there were not only more diagnoses of "nervousness" in America, but there was also a striking class-related issue related to these the diagnoses: "Therefore, while recent immigrants and the poor went insane, members of the upper middle class most often became 'nervous'" (117). Essentially, the identification process of an illness in the nineteenth century also succumbed to a social construction. Not only were women like Beret objectified with a pejorative label, but also her entire class of immigrants.

Bachelard's discussion of the image and role of the house can be connected to the interaction that Beret and other pioneer women had with the house, specifically during the harsh seasons. Theoretically, pioneering women gravitated toward, and found solace in, enclosed spaces of the domestic home. Bachelard's theories seem to corroborate the historical assigned roles of women as he discusses the house in winter.

> This absence of struggle is often the case of the winter houses in literature. The dialectics of the house and the universe are too simple, and snow, especially, reduces the exterior world to nothing rather too easily. It gives a single color to the entire universe which, with the one word, snow, is both expressed and nullified for those who have found shelter. [. . .]
>
> Inside the house, everything may be differentiated and multiplied. The house derives reserves and refinements of intimacy from winter; while in the outside world, snow covers all tracks, blurs the road, muffles every sound, conceals all colors. (40)

Unfortunately, what Bachelard deems true for the imagination does not apply to Beret's situation as she experiences only a limited amount of positive feminine space inside the house. Rather, Rölvaag's description of the general reaction to the snowfall on the day before Christmas Eve echoes Beret's state of infelicity: "Still weather, and dry, powdery snow. . . . Murk without, and leaden dusk in the huts. People sat oppressed in the somber gloom" (232). What most people would consider a festive time of year—Christmas—serves only as a time of "gloom." Clearly, the outside spaces cannot be quickly dismissed with the onset of snow.

Bachelard's discussion about the image of the house provides a possible explanation for the root of Beret's insanity.[9] He says, "The house, the cellar, the deep earth, achieve totality through depth" (23); unfortunately for Beret, this totality comes in a negative fashion as she feels both the natural and manmade environments smothering her. Not

[9] Interestingly, Mary Ellen Snodgrass reports that Johan Bojer's *The Emigrants* (1924), which features a Norwegian migration similar to Rölvaag's, shows a man's insanity instead of the woman's: "On his return with proof that others favor their experiment, he encounters more troubles. Per Foll, who finds his wife entertaining a bachelor and falls into a 'fit of the sulks,' wanders the wild and is reduced to insanity" (38).

only does she suffer from the smothering, but Beret's lack of felicitous space results in extreme solitude in the same vein as Bachelard's image of the "hermit's hut," which "immediately becomes centralized solitude" (32). Annette Kolodny's *The Land Before Her: Fantasy and Experience of the American Frontiers, 1630-1860* discusses women's solitude and isolation. She provides an excerpt of a letter from a pioneer woman and analyzes the social isolation implied:

> Responding to women's reluctance to exchange comfortable household arrangements for primitive conditions—"I miss many of the conveniences of home," Elisabeth Adams admitted in a letter to her sister—the domestic fictionists hinted at a speedy transition from original log cabin to framed house or charming cottage. The fear of geographical isolation to which Elisabeth Adams gave voice soon after her arrival in Iowa—"I am alone tonight, the wind sounds so mournful and the house is so still that I am almost sad"—called forth other devices. (173-74)

What Kolodny alludes to is not as much the dissatisfaction with the lack of technological conveniences as with the sadness of isolation.[10] Beret's dissatisfaction with the sod house and the oppressive winds outside is evident as she grapples with her guilt of premarital sex and the nostalgic, migrant identity of her longing for her homeland across the Atlantic Ocean.

---

[10] Snodgrass reports about Louis L'Amour's similar representation of a lonely woman in *Conagher* (1964). Evie Teale

> expresses her yearning in an innovative form of creative writing: she composes a scattered diary on strips of paper and ties them to tumbleweeds. One of her most poignant lines describes the constraints of isolation: 'Sometimes when I am alone I feel I will die if I do not talk to someone, and I am alone so much.' (176)

Also, Robert Thacker notes that Hamlin Garland's *The Moccasin Ranch: A Story of Dakota* (1909) shows a woman, Blanche Burke, who highly resembles Beret. Blanche goes crazy listening to the prairie wind (134-39).

More importantly, Bachelard's mention of "inverting daydreams and reality" (40) is a significant segue into the discussion of how Beret's insanity corresponds to literary space and memory. In his discussion of houses and related images, Bachelard also mentions Henri Bergson, a reference that seems to suggest a connection between Beret's infelicity and insanity—from the dialectics of space that Bachelard describes—and the incongruity of reality and dreams—that Bergson details in his discussion on memory. Bergson talks about how

> the mind travels unceasingly over the interval comprised between its two extreme limits, the plane of action and the plane of dream. Let us suppose that we have to make a decision. Collecting, organizing the totality of its experience in what we call its character, the mind causes it to converge upon actions in which we shall afterwards find, together with the past which is their matter, the unforeseen form which is stamped upon them by personality; but the action is not able to become real unless it succeeds in encasing itself in the actual situation, that is to say, in that particular assemblage of circumstances which is due to the particular position of the body in time and space. (172)

Beret's specific position and condition around October is one of despondency, lethargy, and unconventional behavior. That "she was always losing the commonest objects—completely losing them, though they were right at hand" (Rölvaag 211)—reinforces Per's suspicion of her sanity: "He tried to wave the truth aside—to deny the plain facts; [. . .] nothing but trifles—things that were always likely to happen under such circumstances! . . . Oh no! There was no danger that Beret couldn't stand her watch; things would right themselves when the time came" (Rölvaag 211). To the reader, Per's hasty denial seems to cast Beret's behavior into Bergson's latter category—that of living entirely on the dream plane. The bizarre switching of her boys seems more like a dream sequence recounted by the narrator who writes that "there was such a strange, unnatural look in her eyes!" (Rölvaag 184).

Bergson continues his discussion of mind, memory, and behavior when he says, "The activity of the mind goes far beyond the mass of accumulated memories [. . .]; but these sensations and these movements condition what we may term our *attention to life*, and that is why everything depends on their cohesion in the normal work of the mind, as in a pyramid which should stand upon its apex" (173). Rölvaag shows the unraveling of cohesion in Beret's mind in scenes like the wild switching of her boys, where, in the words of Bergson, "everything happens as if attention detached itself from life. Dreams and insanity appear to be little else than this" (174). It is notable that Beret has essentially detached herself from life by the time Per Hansa kindly addresses Beret's inattention to personal appearance and nutrition (Rölvaag 210, 209).

As the days progress, Beret's inner spirit becomes more crushed, more constricted within the contracted, inside space of the sod house. The masculine, open space continues to infiltrate Beret's inner space and territory: "Beret stared at the earthen floor of the hut and saw only night round about her. Yes . . . she faced only darkness. She tried hard, but she could not let in the sun" (233). The darkness of the open prairie, the very element of the vastness that terrorizes her, is the only thing she can see now. After another momentary wave of sanity with her childbirth of Peder Victorious, Beret sinks deeper within herself and into her assigned contracted space, oppressed by the ever-invading open space visible through the object of the window: "The window faced the east and they were going eastward, but she could not bring herself to look out. . . . But what she felt was not exactly fear—was not the same fear that had gripped her the time before when he had left her alone. . . . This was a sense of powerlessness" (267). This sense of powerlessness, this yielding to the masculine open spaces, restricts Beret from even looking at the window, her very vision controlled by the masculine forces. The fear and powerlessness continue: every "evening, now, whether Per Hansa was away or at home, she hung something over the windows—it helped shut out the fear" (332). It seems in vain she tries to shut out the fear by blinding an object that typically allows vision, especially when her confinement inside the house gives her no solace.

The immigrant chest that Beret cherishes serves as the best example of the multiple layering of objectification. The culmination of Beret's inability to find a felicitous space results from arguably the most terrifying element produced by the vastness of the outside in Rölvaag's novel—even more terrifying than the plague of darkness—the plague of locusts. First perceived as a snowstorm, it represents the harshest form of masculine force in the open prairie, ravaging even the vast prairie and oppressing both open and contracted space. As the plague gradually subsides, Per Hansa looks for his wife in the sod house but cannot get past the front door because of an object obstructing the way. Per Hansa, the most masculine character in the novel, cannot easily move from the vast, masculine space of the prairie into the closed, feminine space of the house: "Pulling himself together, he shoved against the door with all his strength—shoved until red streaks were flashing before his eyes" (348). After a struggle, he arrives inside Beret's domestic domain, but he cannot find her. Soon he discovers that Beret's chest was the object that impeded his entrance into the closed, feminine space: "Per Hansa flung the cover open with frantic haste. [. . .] Down in the depths of the great chest lay Beret, huddled up and holding the baby in her arms" (348). Beret's hiding in the chest shows the remarkable depths to which Beret will go to get away from the overwhelming presence of the invading masculine space. She believes the best way to defend herself against the vastness is not only to curl herself in the tightest ball physically possible, but also to place herself in the tightest place possible, to constrict herself within a closed space within the sod house, to embrace her feminine, closed space.

Bachelard says:

> And if we want to determine man's being, we are never sure of being closer to ourselves if we "withdraw" into ourselves, if we move toward the center of the spiral; for often it is in the heart of being that being is errancy. Sometimes, it is in being outside itself that being tests consistencies. Sometimes, too, it is close in, as it were, on the outside. Later, I shall give a poetic text in which the prison is on the outside. (215)

Beret withdraws into herself as a reaction against the terror she feels from the open spaces outside her house. In a way, her prison is on the outside, as though she is stranded not by a sea of water, but by a sea of grass. Related to Beret's inability to function is Bachelard's idea that "the dialectics of outside and inside is supported by a reinforced geometrism, in which limits are barriers" (215). For Beret, the vast open prairie serves as a mental barrier. She constantly grieves about a lack of something to hide behind.

The significance of Beret's immigration chest can be amplified through Bachelard's discussion of imagination and memory as well. Bachelard notes, "Bergson shows the indigence of the image according to which there exist 'here and there in the brain, keep-sake boxes that preserve fragments of the past'" (76). For Beret, the chest becomes a literal "keep-sake" box, a fragment of the past. The big chest is an important source of memory for Beret, a sign of happier times:

> It worried her to know where he would find material for a coffin. [. . .] If he could only spare her the big chest! . . . Beret fell to looking at it, and grew easier in her mind. . . . That chest had belonged to her great-grandfather, but it must have been in the family long before his day; on it she could make out only the words 'Anno 16—' . . . the rest was completely worn away. Along the edges and running twice around the middle were heavy iron bands. . . . Beret would go looking at the chest—would lift the lid and gaze down inside. . . . Plenty

> of room in there, if they would only put something under her head and back! (Rölvaag 230)

Beret's chest, a possible casket, signifies her past, a potential felicitous life she could be living in Norway in the present; as Bachelard notes, the casket is an image where "the past, the present and a future are condensed. Thus the casket is memory of what is immemorial" (Bachelard 84). Beret's insanity becomes a result of suffocating enclosed spaces of the house and the unraveling cohesion of mind and memory. Ingeborg R. Kongslien "believes that what Beret experienced in *Giants in the Earth* was shaped by her life as an uprooted immigrant, not a staging of Rölvaag's religious ideas as other critics have asserted" (Gulliksen 191; Gulliksen refers to Kongslien's 1989 *Draumen om fridom og jord: Ein studie i skandinaviske emigrantromaner*). An uprooted immigrant in the spirit of Braidotti's migrant identity, Beret's social construction becomes complete in the chest, making her, as June Underwood says, "the classic case of madness on the Plains. She is frightened by the new life and feels its threats as punishment. She goes into a depression, not caring for her appearance, withdrawing from her family and their meager social life" (55).

Bachelard quotes a prose-poem by Henri Michaux, which begins, "Space, but you cannot even conceive the horrible inside-outside that real space is" (216); Bachelard further expounds upon this prose-poem with words that recall Beret's mental condition: "And we are in hell, and a part of us is always in hell, walled-up, as we are, in the world of evil intentions" (217). For Beret, Per Hansa's constructed sod house serves as both her place of refuge and prison, a walled-up hell of confinement. Jeannie McKnight's discussion about women on the prairie frontier concerns this same sort of hell: "The landscape itself became part of those conditions [that drove pioneer women insane]—consider, for instance, Beret Hansa [. . .] for whom the windy and brooding Great Plains were an eerie kind of hell" (26). And Curtis D. Ruud recognizes the importance land and outside space play in Beret's character when he says "land is important, not only in determining the social stance of *Giants*, in the revealing of psychological insights in the novel, but also in interpreting each major character as he or she attempts to come to terms with the prairie" (217). Sadly, Beret cannot come to terms with the prairie, and the open spaces of the land act as the driving force keeping her from discovering a felicitous space. Doreen Massey's idea of space, gender, and social construction recaps Beret's condition and also segues into the condition described by Laura Ingalls Wilder, which is treated in the next chapter. According to Massey, "there are other ways, too, in which space and place are important to the construction of gender relations and in struggles to change them" (179). After providing a few ways in which this space and place determine "gender relations," Massey seems to echo Geyh's sentiments about the politically charged aspects of space mentioned in the previous chapter when she notes how both space and place "reflect and affect the ways in which gender is constructed and understood. The limitation of women's mobility, in terms both of identity and space, has been in some cultural contexts a crucial means of subordination" (179). For both Beret and Laura, this immobility assigned through gender is conveyed through contracted space. Unlike Laura, who can wander through gender spaces with a child-like naïveté, Beret remains inside, socially confined.

3. Expanding Bachelard's Dialectic of Outside/Inside to Redefine Feminine Spatiality in *Little House on the Prairie*

Perhaps Wilder's most famous book from the Little House series, *Little House on the Prairie*, describes a year in the life of the Ingalls family as they move from the Wisconsin territory into the Kansas territory in the early 1870s. Focalized through the character Laura, the family's story is filled with hardships as they struggle to build and protect their house from the forces of nature.

Wilder has crafted *Little House on the Prairie* as a zone where differing borders meet and interact. Susan Naramore Maher comments that in "the world of children's literature, growing up itself proves a crossing of borders. Young protagonists negotiating the increasing complexities of life face uncertain thresholds" (130). Indeed, Laura Ingalls represents just such a character. From the beginning of the book, Laura must learn how to accept change as her family moves from Wisconsin to the Kansas territory. Part of this change involves discovering her role in the vastness of the prairie. Gaston Bachelard's dialectics of outside/inside can help readers understand how Laura redefines the concept of feminine spatiality. This dialectic can be connected to the feminist issue of subject/object and how space affects this binary. As I have explained earlier by citing Doreen Massey, the social construction of identity can depend on space. Massey says, "space and place are important to the construction of gender relations and in struggles to change them. [. . .] The limitation of women's mobility, in terms both of identity and space, has been in some cultural contexts a crucial means of subordination" (179). For Laura's cultural context as well as for women in this historical period, gender subordination and subsequent spatial allocation are commonplace. Political matters and family matters alike were assigned for a specific gender to decide, even ones about moving West. As Annette Kolodny notes,

> By the middle of the nineteenth century, Americans had to struggle to preserve their shared self-image as a nation of independent yeoman farmers. Everywhere there was the inescapable evidence of an increasingly industrial urbanization made possible by a technology forged of steam and iron. Though the collective mind's eye anxiously looked toward an expanding agrarian west, as though in confirmation of the original eighteenth-century dream, contemporary reality betrayed a growing centripetal movement toward the town, the factory, and the city. (*Land Before Her* 161)

This passage reflects Pa's growing desire to be away from the city dwellers. Though Kolodny believes the majority were moving towards the cities, her passage still supports the notion that towns were getting bigger, and rural places near the east were growing smaller. Pa's impetus to move at the beginning of the novel comes from his ever-increasing claustrophobia from incoming settlers.

Little House on the Prairie shows intersections of various borders. For example, Wilder depicts the interaction between man and nature the night before the Ingalls family moves into the new home on the prairie. The family listens to the song of the nightingale in silence for a moment before Pa plays "the nightingale's song. The nightingale answered him. The nightingale began to sing again. It was singing with Pa's fiddle" (*Little House* 70). In this beautiful scene intertwining man and nature, Wilder leaves the reader fascinated with how the "bird and the fiddle were talking to each other in the cool night under the moon" (70). In another scene, Wilder presents the intersection between sound and silence. One day out in the prairie, Laura listens to the sounds and songs of the wind, grasshoppers, and buzzing from the trees in the creek. Oddly enough, "all these sounds made a great, warm, happy silence" (49), a paradox that makes an interesting connection between two borders.

The prairie also provides a dichotomy between safety and danger. As Hamida Bosmajian remarks, "The value of the prairie's vastness changes throughout the book" (53). Geographically speaking, the prairie contains few trees and therefore few obstacles for Pa as he hunts for game. Yet, the prairie furnishes minimal defense against the natural elements as well. One afternoon "the wind blew fiercely and it was cold. Ma called Mary and Laura into the house" (201). However, even though the house offers safety from the weather, it is not immune from danger. In this same scene, Wilder describes how the "whole top of the chimney was on fire" and the "sticks that made it were burning up" (202), thereby showing the potential for danger even inside the Ingalls' house. Not only does the Ingalls family fight indoor fire, but Bosmajian notes that they must also face "Wolves, [prairie] fire, and Indians [that] can suddenly emerge as real dangers" (55).

Connected to these dangers is the fear of social isolation. Soon after the chimney fire incident, Pa leaves to buy supplies at the nearest town. Ma tells Pa, "'And Charles, I'd like to write to the folks in Wisconsin. If you mail a letter now, they can write this winter, and then we can hear from them next spring'" (206). No doubt, Ma has exciting and terrifying[11] news of their experiences to share with her family so far away. Also, writing gives her a chance for social interaction in a place largely without any. Kolodny's example in *The Land Before Her* of an isolated woman bears significance here: "When Elisabeth Adams wrote from Iowa to her sister in Ohio, in 1846, complaining that 'if I could only have mother or a sister here I should be very glad,' she testified to women's general distress at family separations—and to their particular distress at isolation from female relatives" (173). This coincides with Ma's unsettling feeling of being in the open prairie—a spatial entity that not only feeds her fears of potential dangers, but

[11] Though Ma never succumbs to insanity like Beret, she never feels completely comfortable on the prairie either. William T. Pilkington mentions a character similar to Ma from Conrad Richter's *The Sea of Grass* (1937): "Lutie never adjusts to life on

also divides her from the security of her extended family she once enjoyed in Wisconsin.

Arguably the most important border element in Wilder's book is space, the contrast of the outside and the inside. In *The Poetics of Space*, Gaston Bachelard discusses at great length the dialectics of outside space versus inside space. In his chapter on "intimate immensity," Bachelard says:

> Immensity is within ourselves. It is attached to a sort of expansion of being that life curbs and caution arrests, but which starts again when we are alone. As soon as we become motionless, we are elsewhere; we are dreaming in a world that is immense. Indeed, immensity is the movement of a motionless man. It is one of the dynamic characteristics of quiet daydreaming. (184)

With his first sentence Bachelard establishes a conflict within the very individual, thus placing the dialectic on a personal level as a struggle within the human being. By doing so, he establishes a paradox of sorts: for one's imagination to be immense, one must be intimate; or to experience movement, one must stand still. To a little girl, this seeming contradiction can only promote confusion. In Laura's case, this confusion comes during her simultaneous experience of the immense vastness of the prairie and the closed intensity of domestic life. Maher notes, "Space, at first, daunts Laura" (132). As the family travels, Laura notices that all "around the wagon there was nothing but empty and silent space. Laura didn't like it" (7). However, as Laura becomes more exposed to prairie life, she understands the joy of open spaces.[12] During their journey, Laura listens to all the sounds of the

---

the plains. She is too civilized and refined to accept the raw country or her husband's ways" (383).

[12] Robert Thacker notes that Arthur Stringer's novels, *The Prairie Wife* (1915), *The Prairie Mother* (1920), and *The Prairie Child* (1922), show a woman, Chaddie McKail, who changes her mind about the prairie just like Laura does. An interesting

immense prairie and decides that she "had never seen a place she liked so much as this place" (49). Bachelard's statement that "Faced with a quiet world, on a soothing plain, mankind can enjoy peace and repose" (Bachelard 208) can be used to describe Laura's positive sentiments of the prairie. Nevertheless, once the Ingalls family begins to settle into the house on the open prairie, Laura must face the dichotomy between outside and inside. Bachelard comments that "outside and inside form a dialectic of division" (Bachelard 211), a division that matches Laura's experience crossing into the vastness of the prairie while negotiating having to conduct herself as a young lady in the intimacy of the house. Annette Kolodny's earlier work, *The Lay of the Land,* discusses conflict with nature that relates to Laura's situation. There, Kolodny focuses on the challenges that writers living in the 1800s faced when thinking about "the meaning of their landscape," a challenge that caused what she calls one of the "eternal human dilemmas":

> For, just as the growing child must confront and mediate between his conflicting drives for individuation and maternal union, so, too, the American literary imagination found itself forced to choose between a landscape that at once promised total gratifications in return for passive and even filial responses and yet, also, apparently tempted, even invited, the more active responses of impregnation, alteration, and possession. As the tide of emigration pushed westward and the continent became better known, the dilemma became even more acute: each new settlement repeated the eighteenth-century pattern of confused and conflicting responses followed by frustration. (71)

---

connection to Beret, Thacker says, "Like Garland, Stringer sees nature and human nature as related, and both suggest that the cause of tragedy is confinement" (140).

Charles Ingalls' experience settling in the Kansas Territory coincides with the latter part of Kolodny's statement here. Throughout the course of the novel, Charles impregnates the land with gardens and crops for his family to use. For the Ingalls family, frustration comes near the end of the novel, when they find themselves evicted because of territory dispute, almost as if the land has the last laugh.[13] The part of Kolodny's excerpt referring to the dilemma of the child can be applied specifically to Laura's dynamic character. The obvious family dynamics pair Ma and Mary as expressing feminine commonalities, with Pa and Laura sharing a love for the masculine outdoors. Indeed, Laura is torn between her independence and her respect for her mother's parental control. For example, when Pa constructs the door, Wilder lets the reader know that "Laura helped wash the dishes and make the beds, but that day Mary minded the baby. Laura helped Pa make the door. Mary watched, but Laura handed him his tools" (100). What this passage shows is how Laura, through the lens of Kolodny's statement, "confront[s] and mediate[s] between h[er] conflicting drives for individuation and maternal union" (71). Laura does help out with the domestic chores, but she also is proactive in constructing an object for the house. Interestingly enough, the vast, open prairie plays a part in her identity challenge, serving as part of the temptation for her to shun her more feminine, enclosed side.

For Laura, the exposure to border crossings from her father and the world provides a catalyst for the beginning of her transition into a redefined feminine role, one that transcends the house, the traditional representation of femininity. As Bosmajian notes, *Little House on the Prairie* is a "daughter's fictionalized memory of her father's anticipations expressed through a phenomenology of the spaces of vastness and contractions: the prairie and the little house" (52). Keep in mind Fuss' passages from *The Sense of the Interior* when she says that the "historical conflation of subject and object [is] another binary yet to

[13] I'd like to recall again Diana Fuss' *The Sense of an Interior* as quoted above on page 23 because of her discussion of the theoretical nature of anthropomorphism.

be adequately challenged in cultural criticism" (15). The issue of constructed space and the relationship between subject and object is something Laura witnesses through her father. She sees him construct a home (contracted space) out of materials found around the prairie (vast space), and through this observation of her father's construction and through his masculine training, Laura discovers not only the interconnection between the works of man and the world, but also her redefined role as a frontier girl. Again, the construction of the door to the house serves as an excellent example of this. Wilder notes that Pa "set the door in place again, and Laura stood against it to hold it there, while Pa fastened the hinges to the door-frame" (102). In a physical sense, Laura is a helper to hold an object in place for her father, yet on a symbolic plane, Laura has served as an aid in the construction of an object that will serve as a boundary/border for the house.

The house, an image Bachelard discusses at length in his first few chapters, seems to provide a different experience for Laura than it does for Beret. As Bachelard observes, "A house is imagined as a concentrated being. It appeals to our consciousness of centrality" (17). The house itself is at the very center of the storyline of *Little House on the Prairie*, an image that instills a sense of family unity as each member works towards a stable life on the prairie. A key to understanding Laura's crossing of gender spheres comes by looking at the image of the door of the house. Notice this thread of objects connecting through each main text: Beret's window, the Ingalls' door, and the pavilion enjoyed by Ántonia are all constructed objects that mirror social constructs. Similar in meaning to Beret's window, the door of Laura's house symbolizes a passageway between gendered spaces. For Laura, the absence of the door and the constructing of a door become opportunities for her to dwell more in the masculine sphere as she draws closer to her father. One night a pack of wolves surrounds the incomplete Ingalls house. To Laura, "The house was safe, but it did not feel safe because Pa's gun was not over the door and there was no door; there was only the quilt" (94). It is only natural for Laura to associate safety with a sturdy door, but more importantly she looks to objects associated with her father and masculinity (the gun) for reassurance. A little while later, Laura's fear becomes somewhat assuaged when she wakes up and notices that

> Pa stood black in the moonlight at the window. He had his gun.
>
> Right in Laura's ear a wolf howled.
>
> She scringed away from the wall. The wolf was on the other side of it. Laura was too scared to make a sound. The cold was not in her backbone only, it was all through her. Mary pulled the quilt over her head. Jack growled and showed his teeth at the quilt in the doorway.
>
> "Be still, Jack," Pa said.
>
> Terrible howls curled all around inside the house, and Laura rose out of bed. She wanted to go to Pa, but she knew better than to bother him now. He turned his head and saw her standing in her nightgown.
>
> "Want to see them, Laura?" he asked, softly. Laura couldn't say anything, but she nodded, and padded across the ground to him. (95)

It is noteworthy that, though Laura is naturally scared of the wolves in the night, she does not respond to the situation in fright. Mary, the book's representation of the quintessential timid girl, hides in fear, while Laura uses this scene as an opportunity to learn what men do for the family in potentially dangerous times. She looks through this construct of objectification. She is brave enough to look through the window at the scary wolves, some of which are taller than she: "But she did not put her head through the empty window space into the outdoors where all those wolves sat so near her, shifting their paws and licking their chops. Pa stood firm against her back and kept his arm tight around her middle" (96). The outside, empty space in this scene is dangerous for a little girl, and even though Laura does take the first step towards the outer masculine space by approaching the window, her Pa prevents her from moving into what he deems perilous space. Throughout the night, Laura remains conscious of masculine actions: "But Pa was walking quietly from one window hole to the other, and Jack did not stop pacing up and down before the quilt that hung in the doorway. The wolves might howl, but they could not get in while Pa and Jack were there. So at last Laura fell asleep" (98).

Because of the unwanted social interaction between man and the world, Pa constructs an object that will serve as a gatekeeper. The next day he determines to make a door because "He wanted more than a quilt between them and the wolves, next time" (100). Throughout Pa's construction of the door for the house, Laura plays the role of male apprentice, a role she will appropriate more as she finds masculine space more comfortable: "Laura helped Pa make the door. Mary watched, but Laura handed him his tools" (100). Again, Mary serves as a contrast to Laura, indicating the limitations of feminine space:

> The door was finished. It was strong and solid, made of thick oak with oak slabs across it, all pegged together with good stout pegs. The latch-string was out; if you wanted to come in, you pulled the latch-string. But if you were inside and wanted to keep anyone out, then you pulled the latch-string in through its hole and nobody could get in. There was no doorknob on that door, and there was no keyhole and no key. But it was a good door.
>
> "I call that a good day's work!" said Pa. "And I had a fine little helper!" (104-05)

Wilder's description of the completion of the door also attests to the *security* and *power* of passage the door gives, and Pa's comment provides Laura the encouragement to pursue her excursion into masculine, frontier spaces. Through her experience in the construction of the door, she perceives a potential masculine construction of her own identity. Wilder notes that Laura had done such a good job helping Pa that in two days' time "he and Laura made the barn door" as well (105).

But just as Laura feels a growing interest in masculine spaces, Wilder also includes some important passages about the construction of the inside of the house—inner, feminine space—from the feminine perspective. Ann Romines recognizes the balance of gender influences in Laura's life when she says,

> The six-year-old Laura of the *Little House on the Prairie* is newly eager to explore possibilities beyond the confines of the Little House, moving beyond the rituals, prescriptions, and intimate nurturance she associates with her mother. She turns, as Lacanians would predict, to her wider-ranging father for language (songs, stories) and space. But at the same time, she becomes more conscious that she is a girl who will be a woman, and thus her place and her territory are with her mother. (68)

To demonstrate the importance of the feminine point of view in the construction of the house, Wilder describes Pa's making a mantel-shelf that, with its contents, will represent and fill the feminine space of the home:

> As soon as it was done, Ma set in the middle of the mantel-shelf the little china woman she had brought from the Big Woods. The little china woman had come all the way and had not been broken. She stood on the mantel-shelf with her little china shoes and her wide china skirts and her tight china bodice, and her pink cheeks and blue eyes and golden hair all made of china.
>
> Then Pa and Ma and Mary and Laura stood and admired that fireplace. Only Carrie did not care about it. She pointed at the little china woman and yelled when Mary and Laura told her that no one but Ma could touch it. (117-18)

The china doll represents the family's stability in parallel fashion to the door. Notice how this doll serves as a miniature display of gender construction. While the door keeps the family secure from outside danger and gives a level of completion to the construction of the outer house, the doll fills the inner space of the house and provides an emotional closure to the family's journey into the frontier, letting the children know that this house is their living space. Commenting about household objects, Bachelard reinforces the legitimate involvement that feminine space plays in constructing a house:

> Objects that are cherished [. . .] really are born of an intimate light, and they attain to a higher degree of reality than indifferent objects, or those that are defined by geometric reality. [. . .] From one object in a room to another, housewifely care weaves the ties that unite a very ancient past to the new epoch. The housewife awakens furniture that was asleep. (68)

Bachelard's comment that we should not be "surprised by the fact that an entity which possesses such great wealth of intimacy should be so affectionately cared for by housewives" (81) is also applicable to the special care lavished on the china woman and other objects in the Wilder household. The house's centrality to the overall storyline of the novel is emphasized when Romines remarks, "Rituals, like Ma's household work order and the family's Christmas festivities, are also an important part of constructing this shelter. Building their Little House in Kansas, the Ingallses are laboring to construct the center of a centered universe" (75-76).

Romines also recognizes the ambivalent reaction the girls have towards the house because "The Little House is Ma's shelter, her justification, and perhaps her greatest danger as well; as the girls can plainly see, their mother is the person most at risk in the house's construction, and she is most endangered by Indian men's incursions" (67). Arguably no better scene in Wilder's novel illustrates the danger the house poses to Ma than the initial stage of the house's construction, when Pa builds the walls. It is interesting to note that Pa initially builds the foundation of the house by himself, the "foundation" here serving a double meaning: the foundation of the Wilder home is not only the physical resting place for the structure of the house but also, and more importantly, Pa himself. It is Pa on whom the family relies for support. Nevertheless, Pa cannot complete the construction of the house alone:

> All by himself he built the house three logs high. Then Ma helped him. Pa lifted one end of a log onto the wall, then Ma held it while he lifted the other end. He stood up on the wall to cut the notches, and Ma helped roll and hold the log while he settled it where it should be to make the corner perfectly square. (58)

Ma helps with the structure of the walls, which seems to imply that she gives her share of structural support for the family as well. However, her help with constructing the wall ends in personal harm. Pa loses control of a log while lifting it in place, and the log falls onto Ma's ankle, injuring her severely. Perhaps some can interpret Ma's injury as a warning about the dangers of crossing gender and spatial spheres. Nevertheless, the fact remains that frontier life often required an amending of traditional gender roles.

To Pa's delight, the prairie promises bountiful game, but he must build a well so that Caroline can have fresh water while he leaves on hunting trips. Unlike Beret, who is at the mercy of a migrant lifestyle, Laura and her family, at the mercy of Charles Ingalls, live a nomadic lifestyle as described by Rosa Braidotti: "The nomadic style is about transitions and passages without predetermined destinations or lost homelands. The nomad's relationship to the earth is one of transitory attachments and cyclical frequentation" (25). Historically, the Ingalls family—at the bequest of Pa—moved frequently in the latter part of the 1800s, reflected throughout the Little House series. At the end of *Little House on the Prairie*, the Ingalls family leaves abruptly towards an unknown destination.[14] From the very beginning of the text, the reader can see how headstrong Pa is in his nomadic wanderlust. Pa surprises Ma by saying, "'I've decided to go see the West. I've had an offer for this place, and we can sell it now for as much as we're ever likely to get, enough to give us a start in a new country'" (3).

Bosmajian recognizes the vastness of the prairie when she says that it "is not only experienced horizontally; it also beckons with upward and downward extension. [. . .] An example of the vertically downward line and its connection with sky and prairie is the well Ingalls builds after the house is finished" (54). Digging the well requires that Pa immerse himself into the intense, confined underground space, contrasted with the immense outside space. Bosmajian comments that Wilder "creates an unusual image of the sky lying in the ground" (55), highlighting the vast space within constricted space. After the danger of losing Mr. Scott to the well subsides, Pa again treats Laura like his little apprentice, exposing her to the masculine art of securing the proper oxygen level for safe working conditions and showing her how to successfully ignite the gas with some cloth and powder (157-58).

Arguably, the realization of an interconnection between outside and inside space culminates in this well-digging scene with Laura looking down at her reflection in the deep, vast well. The digging of the well not only illustrates the dialectic between outside and inside space, but also demonstrates Laura's emergent establishment of a revised feminine space on the prairie. But the fact that Laura's growth is incomplete, limited by both her age and gender, is shown by the symbolism of the door to the well. In describing the function of doors in general, Bachelard notes, "the door is an entire cosmos of the Half-open. [. . .] The door schematizes two strong possibilities, which sharply classify two types of daydream. At times, it is closed, bolted, padlocked. At others, it is open, that is to say, wide open" (222). Wilder describes how Pa constructs a "solid platform over the well, and a heavy cover

[14] For an in-depth discussion of Wilder's circular imagery, see Virginia Wolf's "Plenary Paper."

for the hole that let the water-bucket through. Laura must never touch that cover" (161). Essentially, the door to the well is an "entire cosmos of the Half-open" because of the potential dangers of the well. Not just anyone can open this door, yet those both physically and psychologically capable can enjoy the water beyond the door. Indeed, this door is an unusual passageway from the vast outside to the constricted underground, accessible by a select few in the Ingalls household.

According to Bachelard, "a mere door [. . .] can give images of hesitation, temptation, desire, security, welcome and respect" (224). For Laura, the restricted access to the door could quite possibly generate hesitation. As Wilder says, the door is a "heavy cover," an obvious deterrent for a young girl incapable of lifting such an object. Not only may Laura experience hesitation from the sight of the door, but also potential temptation to disobey her parents, as she does later in *On the Banks of Plum Creek* when she and Mary play in the straw stack after they are specifically told not to (55-60). In moments such as these, Laura must choose between another set of borders: obedience and disobedience.

As Fuss has noted in her works, the conflict between subject and object remained unresolved in most cases for women. For Laura, her involvement in being an objectified gender while participating in constructing objects presents her with her own inner conflicts of identity introspection. More significant for Laura than the hesitation and temptation of the door to the well are the desire and welcome that the images beyond the door bring. Upon looking down the well, Laura notices that a "circle of blue sky lay not far down in the ground, and when Laura looked at it, a little girl's head looked up at her. When she waved her hand, a hand on the water's surface waved, too" (*Little House* 159-60). As Bosmajian notes, "A phenomenological perception of [*Little House on the Prairie*] involves a sophisticated primitiveness that both approximates a child's perception and recognizes the absorption of the oneiric value of images as they are perceived in reverie" (51). Bosmajian's assertion fits nicely with this scene of the well. Obviously, Laura does not comprehend the connection between reflection and reality and therefore believes she has made a new friend in the visitor in the deep, watery space below the ground. Laura's waving at this new image in the well is one of welcome; the wave from the reflection could be interpreted by Laura, in her childlike perspective, to mean a sign of respect, perhaps even encouragement from another little girl who enjoys the vast outside spaces of the prairie. Doreen Massey's comments from *Space, Place, and Gender* support Laura's conflicted feelings[15] on the prairie when she notes, "The intersections and mutual influences of 'geography' and 'gender' are deep and multifarious. Each is, in profound ways, implicated in the construction of the other: geography in its various guises influences the cultural formation of particular genders and gender relations; gender has been deeply influential in the production of 'the geographical'" (177). Just as Laura's interaction with her reflection in the well illustrates her reality and illusions of reality of open space (reflected sky) inside contracted space (the well), this passage of Massey reinforces the notion of Laura's identity and how it has been socially constructed on the prairie. In essence, the outside land has allowed Laura to be comfortable in masculine spaces while keeping her aware of her responsibilities in feminine spaces.

Interestingly enough, two modern[16] women's investigations into border crossings illuminate Laura's struggle with the feminine social

[15] Robert L. Gale's description of Ernest Haycox's western novels resembles Laura in her confusion about her role in the West: "Haycox's West is a man's world, but women have an important place in it, so long as they hold themselves in check. It is wrong for a woman to try to be both female and male (note Debbie Lunt, Whispering Range [1931]), to initiate amorous activity (see spicy Annette Carvel, Trail Smoke [1936]), or to force her man to choose between job and love (consider Eileen Oliver, Trouble Shooter [1937])" (188).

[16] This notion of women and border conflict can be seen in contemporary popular culture as well. Mariah Carey's song, "Outside" from her 1997 album *Butterfly*, uses inside and outside space as a metaphor to explain her conflicted, biracial identity, with lines like, "Early on, you face / The realization that you don't / Have a space / Where you fit in / And recognize you / Were born to exist." Similar imagery can be found on her song "Looking In" from the 1995 album *Daydream*.

space of *Little House on the Prairie.* In *Borderlands/*La Frontera, Gloria Anzaldua describes the confusion and frustration she experiences from her heritage in the Borderlands, a term she ascribes to life around the border between Mexico and the United States. Specifically, she describes life there as an "Intimate Terrorism" where "the world is not a safe place to live in" (42) and that the Chicana is caught "between *los intersticios*, the spaces between the different worlds she inhabits" (42). *Los intersticios* serves as a border space of conflict, specifically for Anzaldua, between the Chicana and the dominant male society. This "Intimate Terrorism" that Anzaldua discusses can be transferred to Wilder's frontier world where the intersection of outside and inside clash, as in the scene where the wolves surround the house.

Perhaps this scene with the wolves demonstrates how the "intimate immensity" turns into a possible "Intimate Terrorism." The immensity and power of the wolves in a larger circle on the prairie draw perilously close to the cozy intimacy of Pa reassuring Laura, so much so that Pa "wanted more than a quilt between them and the wolves, next time" (100). As mentioned previously, Wilder has described the scene through little Laura's eyes as feeling unsafe because the house did not have a door (94). The quilt hung in absence of a door deepens the meaning Bachelard seems to attach to images of the door. This door, like others, provides "two strong possibilities" (Bachelard 222), essentially depending on which side of the door you are on. In the case of the front door of the Ingalls house, the possibilities could lead to what Bachelard calls the "wide open" spaces in contrast to the "closed, bolted, padlocked" door (222) that represents both safety and confinement of feminine space. For the Ingalls family at this time, however, the door provides no such closure. The house itself is made of wooden logs hewn down by Pa, and wood seems to be construction material traditionally reserved for the man.

However, what serves as the division between open and closed spaces for the Ingalls family is a quilt, an artifact traditionally assigned to women, yet fashioned into a door by Pa because of its accessibility and pliability (*Little House* 78). Perhaps if Pa had chosen the material for a makeshift door, he would have used a more masculine object, such as a tarp. Nevertheless, that the feminine quilt serves as the door—the great divider between the open prairie and the closed, intimate space of the log house—demonstrates not only Ma's contribution to the construction of the house but also the feminine power of designating and inhabiting a border space. Laura's first reaction to the wolves is one of hesitation: "She scringed away from the wall" (95). Through the intervention of Pa, however, Laura crosses the border from hesitation to desire and thereby expands her feminine space. Unlike Mary who pulls "the quilt over her head" (95), Laura is intrigued, "nodded, and padded across the ground to him" to discover a fantastic scene of nature in the vast, open space, surrounding the more constricted, feminine space of the house. Her transformation on the prairie develops.

Before Anzaldua contributed her metaphor of the Borderlands to scholarly discussion, Dorothy E. Smith used a similar term—The Line of Fault. Smith's term grew from her experience as a woman living "within the social forms of consciousness—the culture or ideology of our society—in relation to the world known otherwise, the world *directly* felt, sensed, responded to, prior to its social expression" (135). In other words, Smith believes this Line of Fault represents the incongruity between the reality that women experience and the reality sanctioned by men, the dominant members of society. This incongruity reveals the social construction of women and girls on the frontier. In the case of *Little House on the Prairie*, women's reality essentially yields to the whims of men. Bosmajian duly notes that although Pa is presented as a benevolent father, he "builds the house to put Caroline and the girls into it. It is he who decides where the contracted space will be" (58). This connects well with the previous chapter when I discussed Per Hansa's building the house for Beret, when in actuality the house confines her and actually debilitates her with the white-washed walls. Once the construction of the constricted space ceases, Laura struggles to conform to her feminine space.

Both Anzaldua and Smith express a dialectic that can expand Bachelard's dichotomy of outside/inside, extending the phenomenology of spatiality to cover a border space inhabited by women. Pa possesses "a childlike joy in building the house, but afterward he does not really know what to do with it. The house is female space, and he prefers to go to town to get supplies or to sit in his favorite place—the threshold—and play his fiddle" (Bosmajian 61) rather than stay at home. Laura is a frontier girl, required to perform her domestic tasks. Yet, as Maher notes, "Pa Ingalls fosters Laura's explorations—both spatial and intellectual" (131), first through his invitation to observe the wolves at night, then more notably in the well scene where he shows her how to extract the poisonous gas, clearly a job done by men and explained to men. In fact, Wilder notes how Laura assists her father after he has set the explosion down the well when he "let Laura light the candle and stand beside him while he let it down" (158). Concerning contemporary sociological conditions, Smith comments that what "men were doing has been relevant to men, was written by men about men for men. Men listened and listen to what one another say" (137). During the well scene, however, Pa includes Laura in a task more suitable for a son or a male hired hand and thus encourages her to cross the borders both of gender and of space, from inside to outside. That Pa should invite Laura to inspect the gas extraction in addition to lighting the next candle indicates in part the beginnings of Laura's redefined feminine space, one that legitimates her love for the outside.

As mentioned earlier, Pa's behavior and tendencies throughout this novel can be considered nomadic. The ending of the novel is no different. Marilyn Chandler has noted both similar and different ways that the house is portrayed in literature in America and in Europe, one particular difference being that she sees a "characteristic tension in American culture between the project of building and settlement and the romantic image of the homeless, rootless, nomadic hero whose roof is the sky and whose bed is the open prairie [. . .]" (5). This tension can be magnified when considering that the inside of a house "runs counter to the inherent romanticism of some of our most deeply held collected values: autonomy, self-determination, mobility" (5). These issues of autonomy, self-determination, and mobility all generally pertain to the Ingalls family in this novel. When their autonomy is questioned by the United States government, Charles decides it is time for them to move. For Laura, the question of mobility translates into physical boundaries and metaphorical character development.

Through this character development, Wilder presents Laura "trying to negotiate public and private spheres, to redefine gender lines, and to come to terms with the liberating spaces around [the prairie]" (Maher 131). Although Laura feels "disconnected and withdrawn" (Maher 132) at the beginning of the story as she crosses borders, she soon revels in the vastness of the prairie. As noted before, Laura's affinity for the frontier[17] causes her to think that she "had never seen a place she liked so much as this place" (*Little House* 49). Unlike Mary, who "preferred to stay in the house and sew on her patchwork quilt," Laura "liked the fierce light and the sun and the wind," and more importantly, "she couldn't stay away from the well" (151), the masculine scene where Pa and Mr. Scott conduct an intersection between vast and contracted space. As a result, Laura crosses "personal borders into a redefined female space" (Maher 139), one that allows her to simultaneously become a part of the outside and the inside.

[17] Mary Ellen Snodgrass describes another woman on the prairie who, like Laura, crosses borders and exhibits male and female tendencies: Mama Coates from Fred Gipson's *Old Yeller*: "In his father's absence, the boy learns from a tough female who not only works hard but also soothes her children's fears of wilderness terrors." (129).

4. Successfully Inhabiting Hybrid Spaces: Ántonia's Gender Fluidity

Arguably one of Cather's most famous novels, *My Ántonia* is about the immigration and acculturation of Ántonia Shimerda as her family moves from Bohemia to Nebraska in the late nineteenth century. The story, focalized through Jim Burden, follows Ántonia's physical and social maturation through many years of trials, including her father's suicide and her working different jobs in extremely different environments, ranging from a domestic hired girl to a laboring farmhand.

Muriel Brown states, "In [Cather's] early writing, men represent those who are gifted and have sufficient discipline to become artists; women are generally decried as silly, sentimental, not quite ready for greatness" (94). Obviously, Ántonia's character is a far cry from these earlier literary women. While Jim still represents Cather's idea of a gifted and intelligent man, she gives Ántonia the greater talent—the ability to freely inhabit spaces of both genders. Ántonia's multiple gender spaces connect well with Judith Butler's idea of a performative gender. In *Gender Trouble: Feminism and the Subversion of Identity*, Butler asserts,

> The effect of gender is produced through the stylization of the body and, hence, must be understood as the mundane way in which bodily gestures, movements, and styles of various kinds constitute the illusion of an abiding gendered self. This formulation moves the conception of gender off the ground of a substantial model of identity to one that requires a conception of gender as a constituted *social temporality*. (179)

What Butler describes here and in the rest of her passage about social discourse applies to the complex character of Ántonia Shimerda, who—as this chapter will show—roams in and out of specified gender spheres, signified by a performative switch in wardrobe and demeanor. In one sense, Cather does not reveal Ántonia's true character until the last section of the novel when Jim sees Ántonia as a confident individual who *is* aware of her dichotomous self. Ántonia's identity, a combination of masculine and feminine spheres, defies an essentially-assigned space. Rather, her space is self-constructed. Because of her self-constructed, gender-combined space, Ántonia has joint elements of both self and other, which goes beyond the idea of Luce Irigaray, who, in Godard's words, "posits an otherness for women that is self-defined, a difference not to be transcended but to be given symbolic and social representation by and for women" (368). Basically, Ántonia's gender fluidity bespeaks Butler's social temporality and fuses Irigaray's notion of self/other.

Paul A. Olson notes that "the plains writers created nonformulaic methods of presentation appropriate to the heroism of the peasant peoples, of women, and of minority groups" (265), a comment about heroism that can be applied to Cather's Ántonia, a literary character who qualifies in all three of Olson's categories. Unlike Beret, Ántonia successfully negotiates the transition from closed feminine spaces to vast, open masculine spaces and back to quasi-feminine spaces, thus resulting in a hybrid spatial existence. This hybrid existence resonates against and actually modifies the dialectic of open and closed spaces. Mellannee Kvasnicka observes the flexibility of gender roles in *My Ántonia* when she declares that Cather's work portrays "a myriad of appropriate roles for women in a time in which that was not often the case" (110). This suggestion of role flexibility connects nicely to the assertion of Ántonia's gender and spatial hybridity because throughout the novel, Ántonia undergoes various environmental changes which require her to revise her role accordingly, whether as farm-hand plowing outside, a hired girl inside, or a mother who works in both spaces.

Furthermore, Diana Fuss' *Essentially Speaking: Feminism, Nature & Difference* provides insight into the social construction and class elements of Ántonia's gender hybridity. She states, "Retaining the idea of women as a class, if anything, might help remind us that the sexual categories we work with are no more and no less than social constructions, subject-positions subject to change and to historical evolution" (36). During the course of this novel, Ántonia makes a space for herself, especially after her father's death, revolving from inside and outside spaces and constructing a space for herself that defies traditional gender assignment. In other words, instead of a working class girl being confined to an area, Ántonia has chosen to redefine what it means to be a farm girl or a hired girl or a mother. Each time she redefines her space, she makes neighbors in the community uncomfortable.

Cather's representation of Ántonia's use of social construction to redefine gendered space connects also with the issue of identity. Diana Fuss covers this topic in *Identification Papers* when she notes, "Part of the problem for psychoanalysis in addressing this question [finding self-identity through the other] is that identification, a process defined as the internalization of the other, itself eludes the analytic desire for possession and appropriation" (4). As was briefly mentioned in regards to Irigaray's theory, the "other" in Ántonia's case becomes complicated because of her ability to participate on both sides of the gender binary. For Ántonia, identity intertwines with space and the potential construction of gender; thus, her gender hybridity suggests she has combined her identities of the inside and outside into a cohesive, functioning individual.[18]

Cather's narration of Ántonia's childhood begins with a transition from one space to another, but before I can discuss this transition, I must comment on the complex narration involved in this novel. As Lisa Hughes demonstrates the relationship between Cather's writing and Plato's classical literature, she makes several significant connec-

---

[18] Lisa Hughes compares gender in writings by Plato and Cather. She refers to Aristophanes' theory of sexuality, according to which every creature originally was comprised of two female halves or two male halves; the Hermaphrodite consisted of a female and a male half. "Early in our history the gods split these creatures (us) in two, to keep us from becoming too great" (Hughes 53). Hughes' referencing of these sexual spaces provides a richer understanding of Ántonia's gender hybridity as she co-habits inside and outside spaces with relative levels of comfortability.

tions between *My Ántonia* and the *Symposium* with regards to gender and space, including the similar framework of each text and the ramifications the framework places on the overarching emphasis on gender and space. The voice of the introduction to the 1918 edition[19]—which until recently was suppressed (Hughes 51)—belongs to a female narrator, while the rest of the novel is narrated by Jim Burden. By telling the story of Ántonia through a male perspective, Cather symbolizes the struggle pioneer women faced while living on the prairie in a patriarchal society where women were viewed primarily as family facilitators and nurturers. More importantly, Jim's perspective reflects the gender and spatial assignment of pioneer women. By placing Ántonia and her female immigrant friends as the object of discussion and narration, Jim keeps the women "inside" the story and powerless to tell their own. Moreover, in telling her story through Jim, Cather, like Ántonia, occupies a hybrid space by playing a role, and thus filling a space usually reserved for male authors.[20]

Although Cather's story begins in the "present" as the narrator and her old friend Jim Burden meet on a train, Ántonia's story is told in retrospect and from Jim's perspective. It is also important to note, according to Madsen as she applies eco-feminism to Ántonia, that

> she is described and discussed by others for whom her significance is more than that of a simple individual. Consequently, she can become symbolically whatever the other characters wish to make of her; in the case of Jim Burden, she symbolizes the feminine, or feminised, harmony with nature

---

[19] All of my references to *My Ántonia* come from the 1954 edition unless otherwise indicated.

[20] It is significant to note that Jim's unnamed female narrator at the end of the 1918 introduction says, "My own story was never written [about Ántonia], but the following narrative is Jim's manuscript, substantially as he brought it to me" (4). What does she mean by "substantially"? It seems plausible that, while Jim has provided the story, the unnamed narrator has edited or revised the manuscript, exercising a certain level of power through her own voice, thus establishing multiple interesting layers of gendered narration in this text.

> that he seeks, and which stands in contrast to the masculine exploitation of nature, symbolised by her surly brother Ambrosch (135)

Antonia's spatial and gender flexibility will become quite apparent by the time she begins to work for her brother. At the beginning of the central narrative, Jim is moving West to Nebraska to the same destination as "a family [from] 'across the water'" (6)—the Shimerdas. Jim must adjust to moving from the East to the West, from Virginia to Nebraska, but—in emigrating from Bohemia—the Shimerda family is crossing major cultural as well as geographical borders.[21]

In the first section of the novel, both Jim and Ántonia are pre-teens, though Ántonia is the elder of the two. For several reasons, it is noteworthy that Jim's tale of Ántonia begins with their childhood. First, both characters are children discovering a new land—the prairie—that is still in its infancy, at least in relation to pioneer settlement. The first night is uncomfortable for Jim as he travels in a wagon across the prairie to his new home:

> I tried to go to sleep, but the jolting made me bite my tongue, and I soon began to ache all over. When the straw settled down, I had a hard bed. Cautiously I slipped from under the buffalo hide, got up on my knees and peered over the side of the wagon. There seemed to be nothing to see; no fences, no creeks or trees, no hills or fields. If there was a road, I could not make it out in the faint starlight. There was nothing but land: not a country at all, but the material out of which countries are made. (Cather 8)

---

[21] Madsen reinforces this point by stating that Ántonia represents "the fusion of the Old World and the New that is the pioneer spirit, at the same time that [she] represent[s] the confrontation of wilderness and civilization that results in nature tamed and rendered powerless, or 'feminised'" (134-35).

Though later passages about the prairie will be positive for Jim, this initiation into the open spaces is not. This scene of Jim's bouncing across the prairie that first September night is very similar to Cather's memories of her first experience of the prairie, and one can suppose that Ántonia would have felt much the same way. In a 1913 interview, Cather describes her trip from the train station to her grandparents' home in this way:

> I was sitting on the hay in the bottom of a Studebaker wagon, holding on to the side of the wagon box to steady myself—the roads were mostly faint trails over the bunch grass in those days. The land was open range and there was almost no fencing. As we drove further and further out into the country, I felt a good deal as if we had come to the end of everything—it was a kind of erasure of personality. . . . I had heard my father say you had to show grit in a new country, and I would have got on pretty well during that ride if it had not been for the larks. Every now and then one flew up and sang a few splendid notes and dropped down into the grass again. That reminded me of something—I don't know what, but my one purpose in life just then was not to cry, and every time they did it, I thought I would go under. (*Philadelphia Record* 9 Aug. 1913 ; qtd. in Woodress 36)

That first night Jim, like Cather, arrives at his grandmother's secure, cheerful home, but Ántonia and her family have waiting for them only a dark, dank, cave-like sod house—a gloomy setting that seems to foreshadow the Shimerdas' future on the prairie in general and Mr. Shimerda's suicide in particular. Marilyn Chambers comments on this dramatic comparison between the traditional farmhouse of the Burdens and the crude "sod dugout of the immigrant Shimerdas" as a vivid representation of the "inequities of immigration, expansion, and land acquisition and the desperation born of the failed hopes and shattered visions of many settlers for whom the great undomesticated land proved too strong a beast to tame" (181). Muriel Brown's analysis of the harsh land connects well with Chambers' as she describes Cather's setting in the beginning of the novel as one that will be difficult for the new settlers to work with and which will take the lives or "haunt" Mr. Shimerda and Pavel and Peter. It takes people with extraordinary courage, good health and physical strength, and spirit, like Ántonia's, to survive and prosper" in this unruly frontier (Brown 100). Brown's description of the criteria of survival on the frontier boosts Ántonia's character into one that surpasses literary men, men usually given the courage and maturity to persevere through such obstacles. Fortunately for Ántonia, the "beast"-land is not too strong for her to tame. At the beginning of their stay in the sod dugout, Ántonia, unlike Beret, never seems to suffer from the claustrophobia of contracted inside spaces.

As shown through his nostalgic memories, the rest of Jim's childhood in Nebraska is relatively peaceful. Fryer's notes about childhood support Jim's nostalgia well when she says that what makes childhood so charming is that it is a "time remembered as less complex, in spaces of vastness, unconfining, yet protective; places recalled seem havens that foster creativity. Childhood is valuable precisely because it is lost, recoverable only through memory" (228). Braidotti's discussion of a migrant identity overwhelmed with nostalgia fits nicely in comparison to Cather's narrative structure where Jim's memories of his childhood in his grandparents' house[22] recall a sense of safety, and his memories of visiting and playing with Ántonia in the open spaces of the prairie (Cather 19) suggest the happiness and freedom that he felt—and that Ántonia experienced for a short while. On one occasion, Jim recounts how Ántonia befriends an insect and places it in her hair, after which "We drifted along lazily, very happy, through the magical

---

[22] Woodress's biography gives more connection between Jim's house and Cather's: "[Jim's] description of his grandfather's house is very probably based on the home William Cather had built. [. . .] In the novel the boy Jim wakes up the first morning on the farm and finds himself in a small bedroom on the first floor of the story-and-a-half house built on two levels" (40).

light of the late afternoon" (28). This passage exemplifies a portion from Bachelard that discusses the dialectical exchange between periods of play and inaction:

> What special depth there is in a child's daydream! And how happy the child who really possesses his moments of solitude! It is a good thing, it is even salutary, for a child to have periods of boredom, for him to learn to know the dialectics of exaggerated play and causeless, pure boredom. (Bachelard 16)

Even though Jim and Ántonia are together on the prairie rather than alone, their experiences have the quality of peaceful solitude to which Bachelard refers. These peaceful scenes contrast sharply with other scenes, such as the time Jim kills a big rattlesnake. However, this episode solidifies Jim's masculinity for Ántonia: "She liked me better from that time on, and she never took a supercilious air with me again. I had killed a snake—I was now a big fellow" (35). Finally, Jim receives the respect he feels he deserves.

One of the first scenes of Jim and Ántonia's developing friendship as they explore the prairie together reveals Ántonia's level of comfort in masculine, open spaces: "When we reached the level and could see the gold tree-tops, I pointed toward them, and Ántonia laughed and squeezed my hand as if to tell me how glad she was I had come" (19). She delights in nature, the trees, the Nebraska countryside, and even the wind that blows her skirts. The openness and freedom of this scene certainly provides a positive contrast to her cave-like home. As Fryer suggests, Jim's understanding of Ántonia is inextricably bound to "images, suddenly apprehended, which become fixed for him against the vastness of the Nebraska prairie—images of Ántonia working, of a tree standing out in the landscape, of the plough inscribed on the molten disk of the setting sun" (291). Significantly, the images in this quotation are all associated directly with Ántonia, and they all occur in open, masculine spaces. Essentially, some of Jim's earliest recollections of Ántonia involve her occupying masculine spaces, acting as a hired hand on her family's property.

Social construction issues deal with many different gender angles, and one that I have mentioned briefly in previous chapters pertains to rhetorical discourse, which is relevant in my discussion of spatiality. This prevailing concept of inside vs. outside and open vs. closed space is as central to *My Ántonia* as it is to *Giants in the Earth* and *Little House on the Prairie*. This dialectic between feminine inside space and masculine outside space will become more prevalent as Ántonia matures and desires her independence. As she discovers more of the open spaces of the prairie, she undergoes a transformation that leads her into hybrid spaces. Hughes' discussion about the relationship between Cather and Plato resonates within my study of hybrid space. Specifically, Hughes likens Cather to Socrates' teacher Diotima for several reasons, notably through the

> interrogation of the system of binary opposites assumed to govern most aspects of life. Diotima has us look instead at places in between so many polarities; between poverty and contrivance, ignorance and wisdom, beauty and ugliness, male and female. Diotima suggests that it does not always have to be one or the other. (59)

This discussion of binaries, especially between "male and female" can naturally take the next step into looking at inside and outside spaces, especially the relationship between gender and the prairie. Hughes goes on to say, "In *My Ántonia* the prairie becomes the physical place where Cather can put forth her female voice, and also exploit these in-between places to negotiate the oppositions by which she is constrained as an American woman writing in the early twentieth century" (59). Ántonia's love for outside space is clearly relevant during one of her early trips onto the prairie with Jim. She desires to attach signifier to signified: "'Name? What name?'" (Cather 19) she asks, pointing to various aspects of nature, wanting to learn new meanings.

It is significant that Ántonia learns the color "blue" by attaching the meaning to the sky—the sky that parallels the endless, open prairie so typical of masculine space. Her level of comfort in knowing the sky and its elements signifies her level of comfort in the masculine world. If, as Bachelard says, "language bears within itself the dialectics of open and closed," with "meaning" associated with enclosure and "poetic expression" associated with open spaces (222), then Ántonia is moving from linguistic to poetic expression, from feminine to masculine understanding. On this same point of vocal articulation, Doreen Massey's discussion in *Space, Place, and Gender* echoes Diana Fuss' notion of social construction and its application to Ántonia, this time through Ántonia's rhetorical discourse. Ántonia's ability to combine gender space through her propensity for language and the masculine outdoors supports a social construction theory rather than an essentialist position that all lovers of the masculine outside spaces are men: "It is a concept which depends crucially on the notion of articulation. It is a move, in terms of political subjects and of place, which is anti-essentialist, which can recognize difference, and which yet can simultaneously emphasize the bases for potential solidarities" (Massey 8). Ántonia's rhetorical power in instances such as proclaiming she can work like any capable man articulates this social construction that will be fulfilled near the end of the novel.

In moving to Nebraska, Ántonia crosses many borders: cultural, national, and—as highlighted here—linguistic. Ántonia's desire to master a new language exposes two qualities of her character. First, it emphasizes her ambition to better understand the dialectic between the English and Bohemian languages, but more importantly, her desire to learn English shows her need to control her environment by understanding names and meanings, thereby crossing symbolically from the inside space of the uneducated female world (where she has been assigned) to the outside space of masculine experience (where she longs to be). Ántonia's interest in acquiring the English language and meaning also shows her desire to engage in rhetorical discourse. Her preparation for interpersonal communication with Jim and her ability to convey her arguments and reasons for working on the fields illustrates her attraction to rhetoric—another out-of-bounds area where Ántonia is not expected to participate.

Nan Johnson's book, *Gender and Rhetorical Space in American Life, 1866-1910,* explores how women were not expected to dabble in rhetorical devices but rather were to adhere to manuals of feminine courtesy. She explains that because women were believed to instinctually acquire a form of articulacy on their own, these same women were "routinely denied women training in oratory and argumentation on the grounds that women had no need for these arts in the home" (54). Yet Ántonia's speech changes and her rhetoric matures, not only because of her ever-growing fluency in English, but also because of her dynamic growth and transition to the outside, masculine spaces. Probably the most notable example of Ántonia's rhetoric comes when she is faced with the decision either to quit going dancing in town or quit working at the Harling's house: "'Stop going to the tent?' she panted. 'I wouldn't think of it for a minute! My own father couldn't make me stop! Mr. Harling ain't my boss outside my work'" (136). Though Ántonia's choices in her "flings" lead to a life-changing heartbreak, her ability to stand up to Mr. Harling's demands and find work elsewhere through her speech shows her gender hybridity, especially during the beginning of her transition to working outside of the home.

Ántonia's interests in every aspect of the open, masculine prairie emerge through her outings with Jim. One significant illustration of Ántonia's fascination with the open prairie comes when she and Jim visit the prairie-dog town "to watch the brown earth-owls fly home in the later afternoon and go down to their nests underground with the dogs" (22). From the open atmosphere in which she stands, Ántonia—with her own dual nature—is attracted to the domestic structure of nature, to the contracted space of the nest within or under the vast space of the prairie. Just as she easily crosses borders, so does the owl, characteristically destined for the air and vast space like other birds, cross naturally into contracted space. At the end of this chapter it is noted that the "prairie-dogs and the brown owls house the rattlesnakes [. . .] because they did not know how to get rid of them" (23). In a symbolic parallel to Ántonia's situation, the contracted, feminine space of the prairie-dogs and owls' domestic nest merges with the vast, masculine space inhabited by the phallic rattlesnake.

Judith Butler's theories of performative gender factor in to Ántonia's actions at this point of her life. Throughout the first autumn, she becomes even more comfortable in the new country, learning both practical and educational information from Jim on the open prairie. Their friendship develops to the point where each begins to trust the other as an equal. Conscious that his gender makes up for his being a little younger than Ántonia, Jim gives her the masculine nickname of "Tony," and Ántonia—again like Jim—runs "barefooted" (27) in an unladylike manner in the prairie. During the Shimerdas' first autumn in Jim's neighborhood, Jim notices Ántonia appropriating more masculine space, a threatening move in his eyes: "Before the autumn was over, she began to treat me more like an equal and to defer to me in other things than reading lessons" (31). That Ántonia should treat Jim as an equal illustrates just how comfortable she is in crossing borders, playing whichever role she feels is appropriate for her situation. Even in the early part of their relationship, Ántonia is perfectly comfortable in assuming an equal standing with Jim during their forays in the open spaces of the prairie.

When Jim visits the Shimerdas' home during the first winter, however, he discovers that Ántonia lives in a tight, contracted space within the closed space of the house: "In the rear wall was another little cave; a round hole, not much bigger than an oil barrel, scooped out in the black earth" (50). In this hole are quilts and straw where Ántonia and her sister sleep. As Fryer says, "The air in the Shimerda's sod dugout is close and stifling. The Shimerda children huddle together in the cave to keep warm" (264). Comparing her hole to that of a badger,

Ántonia explains her comfort in finding heat in a tight space. However, this is *relative* comfort, not *ideal* comfort. Yet in this visit to the Shimerdas, Jim hints at Ántonia's growing masculinity when he says, "Ambrosch and Ántonia were both old enough to work in the fields, and they were willing to work" (51). The feminine images of the cave and badger hole contrast with Ántonia's association with masculine spaces. Living in tight, intimate space can have both negative as well as positive effects, for images such as these can provide security as well as confinement. From the beginning, Ántonia seems aware of the challenges of her confinement, for—while looking up at the open sky above the Burden farmhouse—she tells Jim, "'If I live here, like you, that is different. Things will be easy for you. But they will be hard for us'" (93).

Fryer not only provides an overview of the historical role of the house in frontier life but also comments specifically on the role the Burden house plays in Ántonia's life:

> The nineteenth-century prairie farmhouse was inexpensive, fast to build, large, well-lighted and convenient: it was practical. Unlike a New England hall-and-parlor house with one room for the family and another for ceremonies, the rooms in this house were thought of in terms of function: kitchen, milk room, pantry, living room, bedrooms, piazza. The house was designed for social self-sufficiency: it had to take the place of church, meetinghouse, school, tavern; it was the scene of weddings, burials, business deals, holidays. In *My Ántonia*, the coffin for Papa Shimerda's burial is built in the Burden's kitchen; Christmas is in the sitting room, with the ornaments from Otto's trunk bringing the Old World to Nebraska [. . .]; and it is in Grandmother Burden's kitchen that Ántonia learns the niceties of American life. (276)

Ironically, even though frontier homes like that of the Burdens may have been designed to be self-supporting, the Shimerda house is anything but "self-sufficient," and Mr. Shimerda's suicide[23] serves as the catalyst for Ántonia to seek work and fulfillment outside the house. Jim has already noted that Ántonia is willing to work in the fields, but now that Mr. Shimerda is dead, he has, as Jim's grandmother puts it, "'left her alone in a hard world'" (66), especially since her world is controlled by Ambrosch, a brother who shows very little filial love for his sister throughout the story. Because of the loss of her father, it becomes necessary for Ántonia to work on the open prairie to promote the well-being of her family.[24] As Becky Faber remarks, "Following her father's death she takes on the role of hired man on the farm, toiling ceaselessly in the fields with her brothers" (116).

As one would expect from her changed circumstances, Ántonia cannot study[25] with Jim during the next spring but instead works in the field with Ambrosch. At the age of fifteen, Ántonia has, without regret, traded certain feminine qualities for masculine ones—most notably in her wardrobe—so that she can work comfortably in open, masculine spaces. Her identity becomes more merged with the masculine outside spaces as Shelley Saposnik-Noire notes: "She never goes to school. She becomes merged with the land, identified with it in such a

---

[23] Several scholars have focused on the influence of Antonia's parents. Hughes compares Ántonia's hybridity to Eros from Plato's *Symposium* through similar parentage, each having Poverty for a mother and Contrivance for a father (55). This hybridity is explained in a slightly manner by Deborah Madsen: "Ántonia combines her father's spiritual and emotional sensitivity with her mother's fierce determination to succeed in their new lives" (137).

[24] A similar character in Ántonia's situation in frontier literature is *Tacey Cromwell* (1942) written by Conrad Richter. "Tacey's discipline, self-reliance, and self-effacing loyalty to her family are truly heroic" (Pilkington 384).

[25] Antonia's independent spirit resembles Jenny "Ma" Grier from Walter Clark's *The Ox-Bow Incident* (1940).

> The only available authority figure, Judge Tyler, warns that vigilantism is illegal and that temporary deputation is insufficient legality for their purpose. Against his admonition, Jenny 'Ma' Grier's example carries more weight. A female in men's garb, she espouses a macho philosophy by disdaining churches and sermons and adopting an anti-intellectual stance. (Snodgrass 74)

Likewise, Antonia wears men's clothes and thrives without a formal education.

way that in Jim's mind she is the land; a maternal earth goddess who has the potential to lead Jim back to a new sort of paradise at the end of the novel" (177). Saposnik-Noire believes so strongly that Ántonia's character is tied to the land that she says, "Ántonia's selfhood is carved out of the prairie. The landscape contains her; she cannot exist without it" (178).

Not only has Antonia merged with the masculine spaces, but she has also conformed her identity in an outward, "performative-gender" manner. Describing how much she has grown physically during her first year on the prairie, Jim also notes that she "wore the boots of her father" and "his old fur cap" (80). The dress she wears barely fits her, implying that she has outgrown certain feminine tendencies. Moreover, she is not afraid to bare her skin as she works by keeping "her sleeves rolled up all day," turning her skin "as brown as a sailor's" (80). This comparison of her skin to that of a man reinforces her transition to a masculine role. Normally, a woman, confined to her work inside the house would not have much chance for her skin to darken in the sun. Even more notable is Ántonia's anatomical transformation: "Her neck came up strongly out of her shoulders, like the bole of a tree out of the turf" (80). Jim calls it a "draught-horse neck," an unattractive, manly feature that he associates with lower class women practicing physical labor. Nevertheless, Muriel Brown points out, "Ántonia's vision of what her life could be has been created through hard physical labor and a dauntless spirit" (102), which shows a positive angle of her masculinity.

Ántonia's adept rhetorical discourse reveals to the reader her awareness of what role gender can play in verbal spatiality. Despite the distaste Jim feels for her physical change, Ántonia celebrates her work outside. She likes to brag to Jim about how much work she has done in the fields. When he asks her to consider going to school instead of working the plow, she insists, "'I ain't got time to learn. I can work like mans now'" (81). As Jim eats supper with the Shimerdas, he notices even more masculine qualities about Ántonia: "Ántonia ate so noisily now, like a man, and she yawned often at the table and kept stretching her arms over head, as if they ached" (82). Prophetically, Jim's grandmother fears that "'Heavy field work'll spoil that girl. She'll lose all her nice ways and get rough ones'" (82). Essentially, Mrs. Burden believes that the border crossing from female to male spaces brings negative, social consequences. Jim realizes more clearly the impact of Ántonia's working in the masculine, open spaces of the prairie and her appropriation of a masculine role when he notices that she is consumed with talking about men's topics: "nothing but the prices of things, or how much she could lift and endure. She was too proud of her strength. I knew, too, that Ambrosch put upon her some chores a girl ought not to do, and that the farm-hands around the country joked in a nasty way about it" (84). In regards to her ability to thrive in masculine space, Richard Dillman notes that "Ántonia has the power to transform the land, becoming with her family's help a farmer-artist—a kind of landscape architect in the broadest sense—one who through hard work helps to tame, fence, cultivate, design, and nurture the land" (33). Though Ántonia may be comfortable, even ecstatic about her transition into the masculine space, others, like Jim, do not approve. As the story progresses, the landscape becomes more influential. Saposnik-Noire's discussion of landscape as a viable character in *My Ántonia* echoes Diana Fuss's discussion in *The Sense of an Interior* of the anthropomorphized prairie (14-15). Saposnik-Noire says that the landscape serves as "a unifying physical presence," and has been given a specific "personality" that conveys a certain tone. The characters in the story "enjoy an interactive, interdependent, and at times a symbiotic relationship to nature, so that landscape is not simply a background for the story but a vital personification essential to the novel's becoming a work of art" (171). This symbiotic relationship between Ántonia and the open prairie indeed reflects a renegade social construction inspired by her. She has built a level of comfort in her manual labor in the traditionally masculine spaces. A good example of Cather's narration to show that landscape is not just a background element comes when Jim notes that "The whole prairie was like the bush that burned with fire and was not consumed" (28). This biblical reference aptly conveys this idea of the land being a living entity, almost on a supernatural plane.

Ironically, however, Ántonia is objectified as property by her brother, hired out to work as a man. The second section of the novel, "The Hired Girls," reveals a dramatic transition for Ántonia, a switch from the open, masculine spaces of the prairie to the feminine, closed spaces found in town. At the beginning of this section, Ántonia, still living in the countryside, pleases her brother in any way she can, most notoriously by being hired out by Ambrosch to work "like a man" going "from farm to farm, binding sheaves or working with the threshers" (99). However, Mrs. Burden "saved her" (99) from the masculine fields by obtaining a position for her as the housekeeper in the Harling house in Black Hawk. The discussion of Mrs. Harling's arranging for Ántonia to come work for her provides a significant account of the community's impression of the protagonist's exposure to masculine spaces and Mrs. Harling's desire to transform her to her "rightful" place. Frances Harling notices the unfeminine manner in which Ántonia is dressed when they visit the Shimerdas, for she was "'barefoot and ragged'" (103), a sign that she cares nothing for the characteristic decorum women were expected to display on the outside. However, Mrs. Burden argues, "'unless she's been spoiled by the hard life she's had, she has it in her to be a real helpful girl'" (103).

By the third chapter of this section, Ántonia is dramatically transformed, for she is now described as "wearing shoes and stockings" (104). Serving as a housekeeper in the warm, enclosed spaces of the Harling home, she has reconstituted her attire into traditional, feminine dress. Bachelard's comment that in "the dialectics of outside and inside [. . .] limits are barriers" (215) bears relevance to Ántonia's controversial moves from one occupational setting to another because these settings seem to determine gender roles, and Ántonia appears to test the gender barriers. Despite her movement into feminine spaces and attire, however, she still manages to ignite scandal in town, especially at the popular dances. This third major object that forms a thread through these three whole texts of my study—the pavilion—serves as an interesting constructed object that parallels the female protagonist's social construction. Attracting a conglomeration of various cultures and classes, the dancing pavilion that comes to Black Hawk provides Ántonia and the other hired girls a chance to socialize with men on neutral space, or rather in a combination of both masculine and feminine spaces because the pavilion "was very much like a merry-go-round tent, with open sides and gay flags flying from the poles" (129). The pavilion poses as a peculiar intermediary space for the sexes because the tent has open sides, yet it is partially enclosed by its cover. Although almost everyone enjoys the dances, Ántonia and the other hired girls make a rather risqué impression in Black Hawk society because they dance late at night and would even dance with young men who might have other girlfriends (130). Jim's discussion of the "Hired Girls" in this section is quite fascinating because it conveys the mainstream confusion of women who exhibit more masculinity than the town can stomach. He says that the country girls "were almost a race apart, and out-of-door work had given them a vigour which, when they got over their first shyness on coming to town, developed into a positive carriage and freedom of movement, and made them conspicuous among Black Hawk women" (131). Notice the usage of "race" and "freedom" here. These physically active women who dress fashionably become intimidating to the traditional women of the time, and fascinating to the men. The "country girls" were not considered refined by the upper class women, yet they are described here in Jim's words as having a freedom of movement, the freedom to merge their identities into characteristics of both genders.

The dancing pavilion, therefore, provides an intriguing border space between inside and outside, feminine and masculine spaces. Naturally, Ántonia recognizes the excitement of this border space and "talked and thought of nothing but the tent" (135). Unfortunately, her obsession with this border space causes her to neglect her duties as housekeeper: "At the first call of the music, she became irresponsible" (135). And, "Ántonia's success at the tent had its consequences" (135), meaning that, while becoming the center of *attention*, she also becomes a *distraction* to the men who watch her. Moreover, the border space of the dancing pavilion eventually causes a dramatic change in Ántonia's living space in town. Madsen remarks that the "hired girls are perceived to be a threat to the social order of the town, and the space offered by the dancing pavilion for the free association of all classes of people is especially dangerous" (137). This danger becomes clear after Ántonia slaps a man who tries to kiss her; Mr. Harling makes her choose between the pavilion and working at their house. Her independence and love for the border space leave no doubt of her decision, and her move to work as a domestic in Wick Cutter's house brings out even more feminine attributes in Ántonia: "Tony wore gloves now, and high-heeled shoes and feathered bonnets" (141), a far cry from earlier wearing her father's boots and cap in the masculine open spaces of the prairie. Ironically, while Ántonia's move to Wick Cutter's house does enhance her feminine attributes while serving as a sign of her independence in choosing where she works, it also foreshadows her betrayal by Larry Donovan. Although Ántonia is not physically abused at the hand of Wick Cutter, her feminine space is, for after pretending to leave town with his wife, Wick Cutter returns and invades her room with intentions to rape her. Interestingly enough, Ántonia's escape is engineered by another gender crossing because at the time of the attempted attack, Jim is sleeping alone in Ántonia's room in an attempt to protect her.

But Ántonia faces even more obstacles in her border crossings. After his experience in the Wick Cutter episode and his graduation, Jim leaves Black Hawk to attend the university at Lincoln. The next news Jim discovers about Ántonia is that Larry Donovan has betrayed her and left her with an illegitimate child.[26] Frances Harling notes that Ántonia "'lives at home, on the farm, and almost never comes to town'" (193-94), but Faber asserts that Book IV is the place in the novel where "Cather builds a sense of community for women, a community based on gender and the vulnerability that women in rural areas experience" (117). Realizing that she has been made a fool for giving in to her feminine sense of trust and naïveté, the emotionally vulnerable Ántonia wishes to hide her shame from the stares of critics in town. Symbolically, her position in the gendered spaces of the frontier has come full circle. After being abandoned by Donovan, Ántonia again "'was out in the fields ploughing corn. All that spring and summer she did the work of a man on the farm'" (203). Ambrosch considers her as capable as any man and does not hire anyone to take her place. The Widow Stevens remarks that Ántonia is "'so crushed and quiet'" (203) from her situation, and indeed Ántonia looks for solace for her crushed spirit in the open masculine space of the prairie fields. The clothes she wears during this time of shame also reflect a switch back into a masculine role: "'After the winter begun she wore a man's long overcoat and boots, and a man's felt hat with a wide brim'" (204). During this difficult period, Ántonia places all her strength into her work in the masculine sphere, but the birth of her baby girl awakens—or reawakens—a strong femininity.

In terms of female character development in *My Ántonia*, Kvasnicka believes that this story portrays women in exemplary ways with diverse attributes: "stubborn, loving, weak, grasping, efficient, passionate and independent. They are women who made choices—sometimes difficult ones—and they are women who live with the consequences of those decisions" (111). Kvasnicka focuses on strong women who

[26] In another piece of frontier literature, Hamlin Garland's *Rose of Dutcher's Cooly* (1895) shows another strong woman. "Garland traces Rose's development from her first sexual awakening and shows that a woman who possessed vitality, intelligence, will power, and moral strength could triumph over personal and social obstacles" (McCullough 134).

also work and succeed in masculine space. Tiny Soderball "achieves success in traditionally very masculine roles—traveling to Alaska in a snowstorm via dog-sledges and flatboats. [. . .] The capacity for having adventure, making money, and losing one's zest for life is not limited to those of the male gender—either in Cather's time or our own" (Kvasnicka 113). In *My Ántonia*, Cather provides an example of a woman who dares to use her femininity to achieve the power and control usually associated with masculinity. Kvasnicka asserts that

> One of Cather's most "liberated" women is Lena Lingard.[27] From our first meeting with her, it is clear that Lena is a woman who possesses and enjoys a sensuality which causes her to be stereotyped by upright Black Hawk women. It is also clear that this is a woman who will not be pushed into roles she does not relish. From the days when she is pursued by Ole Benson and his wife Crazy Mary, Lena goes her own way. As a talented dressmaker, Lena, too, enjoys financial security. This independence, both emotional and financial, allows Lena the luxury of being her own person, of enjoying the company of men. (113)

Clearly, Ántonia is not the only woman in the novel who appropriates masculine roles and spaces; nevertheless, Cather's focus is on Ántonia's journey through feminine and masculine space.

Several theorists have excellently conveyed the masculinizing effect the frontier had on women. Ántonia's story ends with her living in a border space. In the last section, the reader discovers that Ántonia has married Anton Cuzak and fulfilled her feminine "duties" as a mother by giving birth to at least ten children (214). Regarding Ántonia's

[27] Another woman in frontier literature is portrayed the same way. Richard W. Etulain notes that in Luke Short's *Hard Money* (1940), Vannie Shore "is a warm, erotic woman who has lived unmarried with a now-deceased mine owner. Although she is an appealing woman, her tarnished background keeps her from being a suitable partner for the hero [of the story]" (438).

character, Kvasnicka believes "Cather presents a superb realization of the traditional role of a wife, and even more importantly, mother" (114). However, masculine characteristics are prominent in Jim's description of her at their reunion: "Ántonia came in and stood before me; a stalwart, brown woman, flat-chested, her curly brown hair a little grizzled. It was a shock, of course. It always is, to meet people after long years, especially if they have lived as much and as hard as this woman had" (216). That Ántonia should appear so *manly* while still conducting *motherly* responsibilities attests to the fact that she is at ease inhabiting a hybrid gender space.[28] Kolodny in *The Land Before Her* notes,

> Perhaps the most tenacious anxiety to which these books responded was the lingering suspicion that women became dessicated or masculinzed (or both) on the frontier. Writing from Kansas in 1859, Sarah Everett thanked a sister-in-law in western New York State for sending dress trimmings. She then added: "It was two or three weeks before I could make up my mind to wear anything so gay as that lining and those strings." "I am a very old woman," Sarah explained, "my face is thin sunken and wrinkled, my hands bony withered and hard—I shall look strangely I fear with your nice under-sleaves and the coquettish cherry bows." The Sarah Everett who wrote those lines was twenty-nine years old. (174)

Kolodny connects this example into a conclusion that is applicable to the discussion of the frontier and its effect on women: "Sarah Everett's fear of growing old before her time, of losing the capacity for feminine coquetry, was a fear that most women (and men) associated with westward emigration" (174). Ántonia's early experiences

---

[28] Hughes mentions the physical comparison between Ántonia and Eros too and makes the connection to hybrid spatiality: "Though Jim is initially disappointed in her looks, still, Ántonia is neither beautiful nor ugly, and so like Eros, she occupies the space in between" (56).

working on the farm after her father's suicide illustrates just how much pioneer work can age and masculinize a woman.

The Cuzack fruit cave, as one of Ántonia's sons points out to Jim, is a cellar made of "stout brick walls and the cement floor" (219), but it is also an enclosed area associated with the feminine space. How Ántonia's children exit the cave fully demonstrates the fertility of this feminine space: "Ántonia and I went up the stairs first, and the children waited. We were standing outside talking, when they all came running up the steps together, [. . .] a veritable explosion of life out of the dark cave into the sunlight" (220). The fertility of both Ántonia and her farm are archetypically feminine, but she also lets Jim know that the "first ten years were a hard struggle" and that her "husband knew very little about farming" (222). As Ántonia says, "'We'd never have got through if I hadn't been so strong'" (222).[29] This statement implies that she also serves as the anchor and provider of the family, using her knowledge of masculine spaces to serve the masculine role as leader of the family.

Probably the most vivid illustration of Ántonia's hybrid space comes from the description of her orchards: "At some distance behind the house were an ash grove and two orchards: a cherry orchard, with gooseberry and currant bushes between the rows, and an apple orchard, sheltered by a high hedge from the hot winds" (220). The orchards exist in the masculine, open space at a notable distance from the feminine space of the house. But what makes this outside masculine space *resemble* closed feminine space is that the hedge closes it in: "There was the deepest peace in that orchard. It was surrounded by

[29] William T. Pilkington notes that Conrad Richter's *Early Americana* (1936) portrays women in a similar light.

> The stories collected in the volume, all set in west Texas and New Mexico, introduce many of the themes and techniques that he elaborated and developed in later works. Six of the nine tales [. . .] focus on the trials and tribulations of pioneer women in the nineteenth-century Southwest. In each of these stories a frontier woman faces alone a difficult and usually dangerous situation; by overcoming the difficulty with fortitude and dignity, the woman proves herself and grows as an individual. (382)

a triple enclosure; the wire fence, then the hedge of thorny locusts, then the mulberry hedge which kept out the hot winds of summer and held fast to the protecting snows of winter" (221-22). The particular description of the orchard's enclosures bears significance to the kind of space the area serves. By keeping out the harsh weather, the orchard stands as a peculiar kind of space where one can enjoy outside weather that feels like a windless kind of inside, enclosed space. Fryer comments that "the form of the novel" acts just like Ántonia's orchard because "both protect the inner space and screen out everything except the blue sky against which one's vision is projected" (274). It is important to note that both Cather's description and Fryer's analysis point towards a hybrid space that brings a sense of peace and completeness. These feelings are positive indicators that this hybrid space is non-threatening and fulfilling, that it provides Ántonia with a place for repose from her harsh working conditions.

As Fryer says, "Seldom involved in the decisions to go West, [. . .] women [of the frontier] followed their men, often with a great deal of unhappiness, loneliness, privation and illness; for them place meant the reestablishment of domestic routines that gave order to their lives" (17). Beret, whose insanity drives her to hide in her chest, serves as a prime example of the kind of woman Fryer describes here. Though Fryer rightly asserts that women have "been denied, in our culture, the possibility of dialectical movement between private spaces and open spaces" (50), Ántonia has somehow found a way of becoming an exception to such a statement by appropriating both open masculine spaces and closed feminine spaces into a unique social construction; in so doing, she inhabits the dialectical and androgynous border space between the inside and the outside. Part of Ántonia's journey is "To find the center of one's boundless desire, to give it form, [and] to begin in a space that is felicitous, one that frees the imagination" (Fryer 293). Ántonia is at home both on the open prairie and in the enclosed kitchen, but she is most at peace in fruitful, felicitous, hybrid spaces like the orchard.

5. Conclusion: The Culmination of Female Frontier Experiences

The previous chapters have discussed various literary female experiences on the American frontier. These experiences oftentimes revolve around the home. Marilyn Chandler's *Dwelling in the Text* "is an exploration of the ways in which a number of our major writers have appropriated houses as structural, psychological, metaphysical, and literary metaphors, constructing complex analogies between house and psyche, house and family structure, house and social environment, house and text" (3). For Beret, the house proves detrimental to her psyche and social environment. The whitewash wall incident supports this: "Her eyes were blinded wherever she looked, either outdoors or in-doors" (Rölvaag 199). For Laura, the house serves as a gateway to a metaphorical gender boundary, and the incident of looking out of the house at the wolves demonstrates this boundary between inside and outside: "Laura clutched her toes into a crack of the wall and she folded her arms on the window slab, and she looked and looked at that wolf. But she did not put her head through the empty window space into the outdoors where all those wolves sat so near her, shifting their paws and licking their chops" (Wilder 96). For Ántonia, the house demonstrates how family structure can surpass traditional gender confinement: "'I belong on a farm. I'm never lonesome here like I used to be in town. You remember what sad spells I used to have, when I didn't know what was the matter with me? I've never had them out here. And I don't mind work a bit, if I don't have to put up with sadness'" (Cather 223).

Through selected historical accounts, this chapter will provide a final overview of historical women who lived through experiences similar to those of Beret, Laura, and Ántonia;[30] in so doing, this chapter will show that the fictional heroines of Rölvaag, Wilder, and Cather as well as their historical counterparts all sought a felicitous space of

[30] For an interesting discussion of frontier women during the 18th century, see Billy Kennedy's *Women of the Frontier* (2004).

their own. A progression of women's voices—fictional and historical—indicates how women have modified their gender roles to accommodate their environment, thereby broadening their potential felicitous space. Beret's character reveals the plight migrant women faced while traveling to the pioneer land and the infelicitous space the open land represents. Laura Ingalls's story shows the social and gender development of women and girls as they adapt to the new environment. Essentially, Ántonia serves as the representative modern American woman who successfully crosses gender borders and finds a felicitous space on the open prairie.

The Frontier Home: A Gendered and Spatial Enclosure

As Dean L. May notes, "both Native American and European societies in North America, since their earliest plantation, have been overwhelmingly rural and agrarian. Not until 1920 did the number of urban dwellers in the United States begin to surpass the number of rural dwellers" (1-2). In other words, the majority of life (not just in the West) in United States civilization until the twentieth century involved families living in rural settings, where quite possibly one family would be miles away from the next neighbor. This rural life naturally entails isolated open spaces.

Historians have remarked about the arduous journey women endured while crossing the American frontier. Cathy Luchetti says, "The westward crossing was an extraordinary undertaking—one that took its toll on the minds and health of women in a variety of ways. For every young girl who saw the crossing as a lark and urged her husband ever forward, there were others who dreaded the endless prairies ahead and the prospect of a future life shut off from civilization" (28). Beret Hansa is one such example of this kind of woman who "dreaded" the journey and potential isolation. As Luchetti's quoted passage indicates, this kind of a journey affected the minds of the women, perhaps instilling a sense of bewilderment and planting the seeds of paranoia as the women wondered what kind of life they could lead out in the middle of nowhere where everything is exposed to nature. Moreover, historians have commented on the peril of the journey, how children in particular were at risk for sustaining injuries by accidentally falling out of the wagon and potentially being crushed. As Riley notes, "Women did not take the loss of a child easily. One woman kept a dead child's miniature rocking chair in the living room of her home for forty years after the child had died" (51-52). Riley's example, though extreme, brings attention to Rölvaag's portrayal of Kari—and brings to mind the nomadic identity offered by Braidotti—the pioneer woman whose love for her dead son drives her insane, so much so that Jakob, her husband, has to tie her down for fear that she will run back to the burial site. The personal loss experienced by frontier women was not limited to the loss of loved ones, but also involved the loss of beloved and familiar places. More specifically, Stratton elaborates on this point by noting that, aside from the obvious pangs of "excitement and anticipation" caused by the movement West, these pioneers would actually be going into unfamiliar territory. She reasons, "In the end, there was the likelihood of no return. These women were to experience not only the initial pains of separation, but the later pangs of loneliness and isolation that often pierced their quiet hours" (24). The isolation to which Stratton refers stems partially from the assigned gender spaces the pioneer women had to accommodate. Because women stayed in the enclosed spaces of the house on the prairie, they felt isolated and without any outside contact.

But the completion of the journey to their new frontier homes did not bring an end to pioneer women's stress. In fact, the move to the open frontier seems to have *compounded* their stress because these women were unclear of how to negotiate the new environment with their prescribed gender limitations. Selections from Joanna Stratton's book *Pioneer Women* provide an enlightening description of such gender limitations. One specific passage provides a fitting account of a woman in a similar position to Beret, specifically when Stratton iterates that women were expected to be in the home during this time period (1800s), and these women filled many different domestic roles. Significantly, "Without full legal standing or widespread educational opportunities, most women at this time could not by themselves escape the confines of home and hearth" (57). For Beret, remaining within the confines of the Hansa house in the middle of the Dakota Territory provides no solace, essentially turning the Hansa's sod house into a prison that Beret cannot leave.

Other scholars have also written about the house and what this specific image means for pioneer women. For example, in their book, *New Space for Women*, Wekerle et al. characterize the house as an object restricting women's advancement in public spheres: "The home remains a critical element of concern for all women because it marks the first hurdle to be crossed in any woman's attempts to expand her roles and overcome the social discrimination leveled at her" (8). Unfortunately for Beret, independence outside of the home is unfathomable. Saegert and Winkel aptly describe exactly what the home means for the woman in terms of gender roles and space: "both a physical space" and a "value-laden symbol" (41). They elaborate on these two definitions of "home" by connecting it to women: "Physically and symbolically the home is a private place, away from the public world of work. It is a place for being with one's family and for sharing feelings, a place to retreat to, both alone and for close relationships" (41). According to Saegert and Winkel, the home is not only a "private space" but also one where the family congregates. This private space turns out to be the only space pioneer women like Beret could call their own. However, as Saegert and Winkel also say, the home is a "value-laden symbol," meaning that the image automatically conjures a specific gender—women—as "keeper" of the home. Ironically for the woman, the home is not a place to get away from work, but actually the place of her work.

This automatic female gender assignment to the home affects the minds of both men and women: "The split between the domestic and public realms and their association with men's and women's spheres of activities maintains a strong hold on our imaginations and perceptions and leads men and women to attach very different meanings to the home" (Wekerle et al. 10). In the Hansa house, Per Hansa is free to roam outside not only to provide food for the family but also to explore his territory and acquire a lay of the land. Beret's perception of the outside prairie is filled with distrust because she cannot hide behind anything, and is therefore forced to stay within her own assigned space. Connected to this distrust, Cathy Luchetti addresses the concept of fear in the open spaces of the prairie when she observes that the historical pioneer women were highly cognizant of their fears, which ranged from Indians to animals to the solitude. Significantly, "Much of their fear—and that of the men, too—came from their inability to read their environment with any accuracy" (28). This inability to respond correctly to the open space relates to Beret's situation in *Giants in the Earth*. Beret finds plenty to be fearful of in the prairie: Indians, darkness, and open space. Riley summarizes the uncomfortable feeling women had towards the frontier: "The prairie frontier, then, was not a particularly hospitable one for women. Given the nineteenth-century role expectations that, on the whole, women's lives would be domestically oriented, women were often disappointed with the setting and the resources that were offered to them by the prairie" (46). In other words, the gender limitations women faced in the nineteenth century often reacted negatively with the new, open-spaced environment of the prairie. Though the women may have enjoyed particular elements of open spaces, they were in little position to truly benefit physically or emotionally from these spaces because of their enormous duties in the house, yard, and garden. This negative reaction to open spaces could also be attributed to the popular conception of the frontier land itself:

> In what must be considered one of the most influential pieces of writing about the West produced during the nineteenth

> century, Frederick Jackson turner's paper on "The Significance of the Frontier in American History" (read before the American Historical Association in Chicago in 1893), attributed to the West the responsibility for virtually every American virtue or vice. In one of his few later papers on the same subject, he made explicit what had always been the experiential truth of the American continent: the West was a woman, and to it belonged the hope of rebirth and regeneration. (Kolodny, *Lay of the Land* 136)

In other words, men's mentality towards the land of the West mirrored their mentality towards women. Both were objects to be conquered and socially constructed as men saw fit. In both cases, men claimed their "manifest destiny." Any "rebirth and regeneration" only pertains to men, and for women like Beret, this realization—that men liken women to the untamed land—was detrimental to their psyche.

The pioneer woman's household chores also added stress and contributed to her overall dislike of the open prairie. In particular, the kinds of jobs women did around the house also worked against their female identity. Jeffrey describes the dramatic degredation the women felt by taking on various domestic labors on the frontier. She notes that some of these household tasks not only took their toll on the women physically, but also mentally, causing them to feel "unfeminine." There is no better visual image to support this than the following: "Since firewood was scarce on the trail, buffalo dung, called 'chips,' served for cooking. Some women saw the dung as the practical solution to the fuel problem. Others found gathering the chips demeaning and indelicate" (Jeffrey 42). Pioneer women so eager to find their place in the open spaces while providing a sense of refined taste on the frontier would have been displeased to perform tasks deemed "unfeminine." During the scene where Beret feeds her children badger meat, Ole, the son, "felt ashamed at the sight of his mother bringing in the wood, though that was not his task; his brother was to be the hired girl!" (Rölvaag 185). With Per away from the house, Beret resorts to providing fuel for the supper fire, even though, as Ole notes, the duty belongs to a boy. Women at risk of losing their femininity because of the arduous tasks expected of them found prairie life particularly disconcerting. As Fairbanks and Sundberg note, it is important to understand that women did work outside of the house, but stayed close by the house while performing a variety of "traditional women's work," such as "raising chickens and hogs, milking cows, planting, weeding, and harvesting the produce from the garden, or shearing sheep" (54). Furthermore, and in light of Laura Ingalls' story, it is significant that "Daughters shared these tasks at home as well as working for other families when the money was needed" (54). It is essential to understand from this passage that, though women were allowed the opportunity to work outside, the region in which they labored was still near the house.

Nevertheless, women still struggled to get a better grasp of their gender identity. I have mentioned before about space and social construction. Beret serves as a literary example of someone disrupted by the open space of the frontier. Echoing Braidotti's nomadic and migrant identities, Linda McDowell discusses how

> This disruption of space through migration [. . .] has parallels with women's position in the West, perhaps making more visible arguments from within feminism about women's awkward 'place' in the West. For women, too, were/are excluded by Western philosophical ideals, equally 'out of place' in that discursive space called the West. The long debate about the public and the private is too familiar to need rehearsal here, but it reminds us of the significance of geographical location to the construction of gendered identities. (39)

That is to say, the relegation of certain space to pioneer women can be argued as correlative to the uncomfortable sentiment those pioneer women feel towards that space.

As Glenda Riley argues, "these shared experiences and responses of frontierswomen constituted a 'female frontier.' In other words, frontierswomen's responsibilities, life styles, and sensibilities were shaped more by gender considerations than by region" (2). Therefore, women living in the prairie around Beret's time suffered from being assigned specific spaces because of their gender. Furthermore, "Even unmarried women and married women who worked outside the home usually found their employment opportunities limited by their gender" (Riley 2). In other words, even if a woman like Beret could find and accept a job outside of the house, she would still be restricted in what she could do. As a result, Beret's insanity comes as no surprise. Like many women during this historical period, Beret serves as a literary representative of the experiences women faced as they lived in an assigned gendered space.

Another important factor to discuss in regards to the pioneer woman's plight on the frontier concerns the way writers portray pioneer women. The differences in the way women writers and men writers deal with the frontier topic bears importance to the overall topic. Responding to Mickey Pearlman's passage that "most American women do not write of open spaces and open roads, rife with potential and possibilities [. . .]. They write [. . .] of the usually imprisoning psychological and actual spaces of American women, of being trapped, submerged, overwhelmed" (Pearlman 5), Becky Faber notes, "How different we would then think that women's farm novels would be from those written by men, where the open spaces, open roads, potential and possibilities and escapes would be at the very core of each book!" (Faber 115). For Faber, the open space of the prairie is not neutral or positive, but instead has a significant negative impact on the feelings of unhappy pioneer women who felt almost imprisoned in their houses.

Riley further documents the plight of pioneer women as represented in pioneer fiction, noting that the

> early tradition of strong [literary] frontierswomen was expanded during the twentieth century by such writers as Willa Cather, Vardis Fisher, Mari Sanoz, and Bess Streeter Aldrich, through their representations of women who displayed great stamina and ingenuity. During the early decades of the twentieth century, this longstanding trend to picture frontierswomen as able and self-reliant received a serious challenge from the works of two writers who had little experience with the West and its women. One of these was Ole E. Rölvaag, who himself never homesteaded [. . .]. Yet, with [his] heart-rending lamentations concerning women's work loads, hostility to the frontier, and tendencies toward insanity, [Rölvaag] etched the picture of a helpless, hopeless drudge into the minds of generations of American readers. (9)

Significantly, Riley contrasts the portrayal of pioneer women by Rölvaag and Cather. While in some ways this passage seems to question the authenticity of Rölvaag's portrayal of women on the prairie through Beret's inability to cope with the environment and eventual insanity, I would argue that this comparison with Cather serves more as foil for Ántonia, who willingly participates in the cultivation of the open space.

Little Girl on the Prairie

In contrast to Beret's plight with the open space, Laura's unofficial apprenticeship to her father as well as Ma and Pa's relationship give her the opportunity to realize that open spaces can be rewarding. The following description could be applied to the parental relationship that Laura observes:

> To the pioneer woman, home and hearth meant work loads that were heavier than ever. And yet that work was the work of survival. In its isolation, the pioneer family existed as a self-sufficient unit that took pride in its ability to provide for itself and persevere in the face of hardship. Men and women worked together as partners, combining their strengths and talents to provide food and clothing for themselves and their children. As a result, women found themselves on a far more equal footing with their spouses. (Stratton 57)

That men and women should combine their talents to keep the family surviving in the prairie suggests that, even though women did struggle in their allotted gender spaces, they still took advantage of opportunities to work alongside men in various ways. Ma's injury during the constructing of the house walls shows Laura that women can work alongside men, especially when the family's survival is at stake. More importantly, though, this passage from Stratton helps to interpret Laura's inclination to work with her father as more than just a desire to be around him.

Several other scholars indicate that women and girls on the prairie found themselves, like Laura Ingalls, open to opportunities to work in masculine space. For example, Riley stresses that if the number of males for a specific task was not enough, it was considered feasible to look for females to fill in the gap: "Girls therefore often joined boys as stock herders [. . .]. In other families, the girls rode horses that were pulling a binder, shocked grain, and helped to thresh wheat. They also hunted and trapped wild game" (53). That Laura should be drafted by Pa to fulfill the duties of a hired boy while he constructs the door and well coincides with Riley's description of the stage of gender development on the frontier. For pioneer girls as well as boys, "Life was not all play or schooling for Plains children, because they were generally regarded as workers in their own right" (Riley 84), and girls who were given the freedom to do men's jobs often "became tomboys"

(Riley 53). Nevertheless Laura's crossing into masculine spaces concerns Ma, for she constantly reminds Laura to act like a civilized girl. Ma's fears for Laura are reflected in Riley's discussion about prairie mothers who wanted to keep their houses civilized; often these "mothers, despairing that their daughters were losing every semblance of civilized womanhood, commanded their daughters to sit primly, wear sunbonnets when outdoors, and use ladylike language" (Riley 53). Similarly, at various times throughout Wilder's novel, Ma politely reminds Laura to speak properly and wear her sunbonnet outside to keep her fair complexion.

Even though Laura is a "tomboy," the assigned gender roles still apply to her and the other girls in the novel. As Ann Romines notes, "As was typical of many nineteenth-century westering women, Ma did not make the decision to emigrate to Kansas. Instead, she acquiesced to her husband's wish" (67). It is important to remember that, though Ma works alongside Pa, she still is subject to his decision. Also, Laura herself, though she has crossed gender spaces and works with her father outside, must realize that her position as a girl on the prairie will not remain the same as she physically matures. As Romines aptly states,

> The six-year-old Laura of the *Little House on the Prairie* is newly eager to explore possibilities beyond the confines of the Little House, moving beyond the rituals, prescriptions, and intimate nurturance she associates with her mother. [. . .] But at the same time, she becomes more conscious that she is a girl who will be a woman, and thus her place and her territory are with her mother. (68)

Through the *Little House* series, Laura conforms to her gender roles and society's expectations and eventually forsakes her earlier positions in masculine space.

The Modern American Woman—Ántonia

The previous chapter established Ántonia as a representative of the early modern American woman. Though a literary character, Ántonia shares characteristics with real pioneer women such as Clara Hildebrand, a pioneer Kansas woman who contributed to the work in "the garden, the orchard, the crops and animals of the farm," had an intimate knowledge about "each vineyard or tree in the young orchard," and "shared in the hopes for a bountiful crop as the field things sprouted and grew green and tall" (Stratton 61). Passages like this one clearly relate to Cather's story of Ántonia, a woman not afraid to work in the fields after the death of her father and in the gardens and orchards as the mother of a large family. Symbolically, the garden, orchard, and fields of crops are an extension of the inside space of the house into the outer masculine world—a felicitous space representative of both genders. Moreover, just as Ántonia worked in the fields after her father's death to help her family survive, Riley notes that "Because both the women and the men believed that the work of the farm or other business that supported the family had to come first, they accepted the idea that women should 'help out' whenever necessary" (62).

However, not all of Ántonia's experience with men and with open spaces is positive. After she becomes pregnant by Larry Donovan, her work in the fields for her brother Ambrosch does not give her the same fulfillment that it once did. In fact, unable to shake off the stark symbol of femininity that her body now represents, she nevertheless tries to hide this apparently troublesome femininity behind a man's overcoat and punishes her feminine body by overworking it. Ántonia must recognize that her ability to work like a man does not negate her female body and its positive potential to (re)produce. The birth of her baby brings this recognition and a celebration of the feminine in her daughter. On one of his trips back home, Jim notices "in a heavy frame, one of those depressing 'crayon enlargements' often seen in farm-house parlours, the subject being a round-eyed baby in short dresses" (Cather 197). This baby dressed in feminine clothing is none other than Ántonia's first child.

After this intense struggle for gender identity, Ántonia salvages her broken life and becomes happily married. By the time of Jim's reunion with her, Ántonia's family is healthy and fruitful, and Ántonia herself thrives on her independent spirit. Cathy Luchetti's photo-text about frontier women gives a striking account of the fierce independence certain women displayed in their new life on the frontier, qualities that seem to describe Ántonia throughout parts of the novel, such as when Luchetti describes their new-found "autonomy" on the frontier that allowed them to "solve their problems in any way they could," and when "'women's work' soon came to mean whatever had to be done, whether it was herding cattle, checking trap lines, or seeding the rows with corn" (31). On one hand, the move West seemed to be a disadvantage to pioneer women because they experienced an overwhelming amount of fear, isolation, disillusion, death, disease, and strife as they were confined to closed, feminine space on the prairie. Nevertheless, Luchetti's statement shows the flip side of the situation and how women could take advantage of a fledgling civilization that needed all the help it could get in order to ensure its success. When she was a child, Ántonia was expected by her family to fulfill farming duties normally reserved to her father and brother, especially after the death of her father; as a wife and mother, her own family relies on her not only to feed, nurture, and love them, but also to provide the leadership in their farm—leadership needed and accepted by the city man she has married.

Ántonia and her childhood friends Tiny Soderball and Lena Lingard are fictional representatives of the women described by Luchetti in the following passage:

> From a society in the early 1800s that had been 90 percent agricultural, women emerged by the end of the century to

> greet the Industrial Revolution with great enthusiasm. For the first time, they had a wide choice of job opportunities, and by 1890, women worked in 216 of the 300 occupations listed by the Federal Office of Opportunity. In some states women could serve on juries, attend college, and receive advance degrees. Some studied medicine or law, some worked in industry, while still others—often women widowed by the Civil War—found themselves with money to invest. Antiquated laws which gave the husband custody of the wife's person and property were amended; divorces were increasing and homestead enactments made land available to single women for the first time in history. (Luchetti 35)

Women just like Ántonia found themselves faced with new rights, new opportunities, and new respect. Ántonia, through Cather, serves as an example of "the breakdown of the binary conceptualization of gender [. . .]. With the binary opposition proved illusory, our attention turns from the poles to that space between them" (Hughes 60). Luce Irigaray's thoughts from *An Ethics of Sexual Difference* are quite appropriate to end this study:

> How can we mark this limit of a place, of place in general, if not through sexual difference? But, in order for an ethics of sexual difference to come into being, we must constitute a possible place for each sex, body, and flesh to inhabit. Which presupposes a memory of the past, a hope for the future, memory bridging the present and disconcerting the mirror symmetry that annihilates the difference of identity. (17-18)

While Irigaray asserts the need for women to have their own space, she does not believe women ought to be relegated solely to those assigned spaces. Ántonia serves as a wonderful literary example of Irigaray's passage because her sexual difference merges the memory of the past—of what a traditional woman was—into a hope for the future, where a modern woman can successfully function in *both* spheres of identity. Women, once restricted to inside, closed space, successfully negotiated the volatile topics of gender and space and were eventually given the right to own land—outside, open space on the vast prairie, where women did not have to wonder anymore if they could find a felicitous space.

Works Cited

Anzaldua, Gloria. *Borderlands*/La Frontera. 2nd ed. San Francisco: Aunt Lute Books, 1999.

Armitage, Susan H. "Women's Literature and the American Frontier: A New Perspective on the Frontier Myth." Lee and Lewis 5-13.

Ardener, Shirley. "Ground Rules and Social Maps for Women: An Introduction." *Women and Space: Ground Rules and Social Maps*. Ed. Shirley Ardener. New York: St. Martin's, 1981. 11-32.

Bachelard, Gaston. *The Poetics of Space*. Trans. Maria Jolas. Foreword by Etienne Gilson. New York: Orion, 1962.

Baym, Nina. "Melodramas of Beset Manhood: How Theories of American Fiction Exclude Women Authors." *The New Feminist Criticism: Essays on Women, Literature, and Theory*. Ed. Elaine Showalter. New York: Pantheon, 1985. 63-79.

Bergson, Henri. *Matter and Memory*. Trans. Nancy Margaret Paul and W. Scott Palmer. 1908. 5th ed. New York: Zone, 1988.

Bosmajian, Hamida. "Vastness and Contraction of Space in *Little House on the Prairie*." *Children's Literature: Annual of The Modern Language Association Division on Children's Literature and The Children's Literature Association*. Vol. 11. New Haven, CT: Yale UP, 1983. 49-63.

Braidotti, Rosi. *Nomadic Subjects: Embodiment and Sexual Difference in Contemporary Feminist Theory*. New York: Columbia UP, 1994.

Brown, Muriel. "Growth and Development of the Artist: Willa Cather's *My Ántonia*." *The Midwest Quarterly* 33.1 (1991): 93-107.

Butler, Judith. *Gender Trouble: Feminism and the Subversion of Identity*. 1990. New York: Routledge, 1999.

Carey, Mariah. "Looking In." *Daydream*. Sony, 1995.

___. "Outside." *Butterfly*. Sony, 1997.

Cather, Willa. *My Ántonia*. 1918. Cambridge: Riverside, 1954.

___. *My Ántonia*. 1918. New York: Bantam, 2005.

Chandler, Marilyn R. *Dwelling in the Text: Houses in American Fiction*. Berkeley, CA: U of California P, 1991.

Dillman, Richard. "Imagining the Land: Five Versions of the Landscape in Willa Cather's *My Ántonia*." *Heritage of the Great Plains* 22.3 (Summer 1989): 30-35.

Erisman, Fred. "A. B. Guthrie Jr." Erisman and Etulain.

Erisman, Fred, and Richard W. Etulain, eds. *Fifty Western Writers: A Bio-bibliographical Sourcebook*. Westport, CT: Greenwood P, 1982.

Etulain, Richard W. "Luke Short." Erisman and Etulain.

Faber, Becky. "Women Writing about Farm Women." *Great Plains Quarterly* 18 (Spring 1998): 113-26.

Fairbanks, Carol, and Sara Brooks Sundberg. *Farm Women on the Prairie Frontier: A Sourcebook for Canada and the United States*. Metuchen, NJ: Scarecrow P, 1983.

Fowler, Rowena. "Feminist Criticism: The Common Pursuit." *New Literary History* 19.1 (1987): 51-62.

Fryer, Judith. *Felicitous Space: The Imaginative Structures of Edith Wharton and Willa Cather*. Chapel Hill: U of North Carolina P, 1986.

Fuss, Diana. *Essentially Speaking: Feminism, Nature & Difference*. New York: Routledge, 1989.

___. *Identification Papers*. New York: Routledge, 1995.

___. *The Sense of an Interior*. New York: Routledge, 2004.

Gale, Robert L. "Ernest Haycox." Erisman and Etulain.

Geyh, Paula E. "Burning Down the House? Domestic Space and Feminine Subjectivity in Marilynne Robinson's *Housekeeping*." *Contemporary Literature* 34.1 (1993): 103-22.

Gilbert, Sandra, and Susan Gubar. *The Madwoman in the Attic*. New Haven: Yale UP, 1979.

Grider, Sylvia. "Madness and Personification in *Giants in the Earth*." *Women, Women Writers, and the West*. Lee and Lewis 111-17.

Godard, Barbara. "Irigaray, Luce." *Encyclopedia of Contemporary Literary Theory*. Ed. Irena R. Makaryk. Toronto: U of Toronto P, 1997.

Gulliksen, Oyvind T. *Twofold Identities: Norwegian-American Contributions to Midwestern Literature*. New York: Peter Lang, 2004.

Handley, William R. *Marriage, Violence, and the Nation in the American Literary West*. New York: Cambridge UP, 2002.

Hautzig, Esther. *The Endless Steppe*. New York: HarperCollins, 1987.

Heilbrun, Carolyn G. *Reinventing Womanhood*. New York: Norton, 1979.

Herndl, Diane Price. *Invalid Women: Figuring Feminine Illness in American Fiction and Culture, 1840-1940*. Chapel Hill: U of North Carolina P, 1993.

Hirschon, Renée. "Essential Objects and the Sacred: Interior and Exterior Space in an Urban Greek Locality." *Women and Space: Ground Rules and Social Maps*. Ed. Shirley Ardener. New York: St. Martin's, 1981. 72-88.

___. "Open Body/Closed Space: The Transformation of Female Sexuality." *Defining Females: The Nature of Women in Society*. Ed. Shirley Ardener. New York: John Wiley & Sons, 1978. 66-88.

Hughes, Lisa. "Gender, Sexuality, and Writing in Plato and Cather." *Classical and Modern Literature* 22.1 (Spring 2002): 49-60.

Irigaray, Luce. *An Ethics of Sexual Difference*. Trans. Carolyn Burke and Gillian C. Gill. Ithica, NY: Cornell UP, 1993.

Jeffrey, Julie Roy. *Frontier Women: The Trans-Mississippi West 1840-1880*. New York: Hill and Wang, 1979.

Johnson, Nan. *Gender and Rhetorical Space in American Life, 1866-1910*. Carbondale, IL: Southern Illinois UP, 2002.

Kennedy, Billy. *Women of the Frontier*. Greenville, SC: Ambassador, 2004.

Kolodny, Annette. *The Land Before Her: Fantasy and Experience of the American Frontiers, 1630-1860*. Chapel Hill: U of North Carolina P, 1984.

___. *The Lay of the Land: Metaphor as Experience and History in American Life and Letters.* Chapel Hill: U of North Carolina P, 1975.

Kvasnicka, Mellanee. "Anything a Woman Can Be: Women's Roles in *My Ántonia.*" *Nebraska English Journal* 37.1 (Fall 1991): 110-17.

Lawrence, D. H. *Studies in Classic American Literature.* London: William Heinemann, 1924.

Lee, L. L., and Merrill Lewis, eds. *Women, Women Writers, and the West.* Troy, NY: Whitston, 1979.

Luchetti, Cathy. *Women of the West.* St. George, UT: Antelope Island P, 1982.

Madsen, Deborah L. *Feminist Theory and Literary Practice.* London: Pluto, 2000.

Maher, Susan Naramore. "Laura Ingalls and Caddie Woodlawn: Daughters of a Border Space." *The Lion and the Unicorn* 18.2 (Dec. 1994): 130-42.

Massey, Doreen. *Space, Place, and Gender.* Minneapolis, MN: U of Minnesota P, 1994.

May, Dean L. *Three Frontiers: Family, Land, and Society in the American West, 1850-1900.* Cambridge: Cambridge UP, 1994.

McCullough, Joseph. "Hamlin Garland." Erisman and Etulain.

McDowell, Linda. "Spatializing Feminism: Geographic Perspectives." *Bodyspace: Destabilizing Geographics of Gender and Sexuality.* Ed. Nancy Duncan. London, Routledge, 1996. 28-44.

McKnight, Jeannie. "American Dream, Nightmare Underside: Diaries, Letters and Fiction of Women on the American Frontier." Lee and Lewis 25-44.

Olson, Paul A. "The Epic and Great Plains Literature: Rölvaag, Cather, and Neihardt." *Prairie Schooner* 55.1-2 (Spring-Summer 1981): 263-85.

Pearlman, Mickey. *American Women Writing Fiction.* Lexington, KY: UP of Kentucky, 1988.

Pilkington, William T. "Conrad Richter." Erisman and Etulain.

Riley, Glenda. *The Female Frontier: A Comparative View of Women on the Prairie and the Plains.* Lawrence, KS: UP of Kansas, 1988.

Rölvaag, Ole Edvart. *Giants in the Earth.* Trans. Lincoln Colcord and O. E. Rölvaag. English trans. 1927. New York: Harper & Row, 1929.

Romines, Ann. *Constructing the Little House: Gender, Culture, and Laura Ingalls Wilder.* Amherst, MA: U of Massachusetts P, 1997.

Ruud, Curtis. "Beret and the Prairie in *Giants in the Earth.*" *Norwegian-American Studies* 28 (1979): 217-44.

Ruthven, K. K. "Male Critics and Feminist Criticism." *Essays in Criticism* 33.4 (1983): 263-72.

Saegert and Winkel. "The Home: A Critical Problem for Changing Sex Roles." *New Space for Women.* Ed. Gerda R. Wekerle et al. Boulder, CO: Westview, 1980. 41-63.

Saposnik-Noire, Shelley. "The Silent Protagonist: The Unifying Presence of Landscape in Willa Cather's *My Ántonia.*" *Midwest Quarterly* 31.2 (1990): 171-79.

Showalter, Elaine. "Introduction: The Feminist Critical Revolution." *The New Feminist Criticism: Essays on Women, Literature, and Theory.* Ed. Elaine Showalter. New York: Pantheon, 1985. 3-17.

___. "Towards a Feminist Poetics." *The New Feminist Criticism: Essays on Women, Literature and Theory.* Ed. Elaine Showalter. New York: Pantheon, 1985. 125-43.

Smith, Dorothy E. "A Sociology for Women." *The Prism of Sex: Essays in the Sociology of Knowledge.* Ed. Julia A. Sherman and Evelyn Torton Beck. Madison, WI: U of Wisconsin P, 1979. 135-87.

Smith, Henry Nash. *Virgin Land: The American West as Symbol and Myth.* New York: Vintage Books, 1950.

Snodgrass, Mary Ellen. "Bojer, Johan." Snodgrass, *Encyclopedia.*

___. "Clark, Walter." Snodgrass, *Encyclopedia.*

___. "Gipson, Fred." Snodgrass, *Encyclopedia*.

___. *Encyclopedia of Frontier Literature*. Santa Barbara, CA: ABC-CLIO Inc, 1997.

___. "L'Amour, Louis." Snodgrass, *Encyclopedia*.

___. "Short Fiction of the Frontier." Snodgrass, *Encyclopedia*.

Stratton, Joanna L. *Pioneer Women: Voices from the Kansas Frontier*. New York: Simon and Schuster, 1981.

Thacker, Robert. *The Great Prairie Fact and Literary Imagination*. Albuquerque, NM: U of New Mexico P, 1989.

Thomas, Joyce Carol. *I Have Heard of a Land*. Illus. Floyd Cooper. New York: HarperCollins, 2000.

Underwood, June O. "Men, Women, and Madness: Pioneer Plains Literature." *Under the Sun: Myth and Realism in Western American Literature*. Ed. Barbara Howard Meldrum. Troy, NY: Whitston, 1985. 50-63

Walker, Victoria. "Feminist Criticism, Anglo-American." *Encyclopedia of Contemporary Literary Theory*. Ed. Irena R. Makaryk. Toronto: U of Toronto P, 1993.

Wekerle, Gerda R., Rebecca Peterson, and David Morley, eds. Introduction. *New Space for Women*. Boulder, CO: Westview, 1980. 1-34.

Wilder, Laura Ingalls. *Little House on the Prairie*. 1935. New York: HarperCollins, 1971.

___. *On the Banks of Plum Creek*. 1937. New York: HarperCollins, 1971.

Wolf, Virginia. "Plenary Paper: The Magic Circle of Laura Ingalls Wilder." *Children's Literature Association Quarterly* 9.4 (Winter 1984-1985): 168-70.

Woodress, James. *Willa Cather: A Literary Life*. Lincoln, NE: U of Nebraska P, 1987.

STUDIES IN ENGLISH LITERATURES

Edited by Koray Melikoğlu

ISSN 1614-4651

1 *Özden Sözalan*
The Staged Encounter
Contemporary Feminism and Women's Drama
2nd, revised editon
ISBN 3-89821-367-6

2 *Paul Fox (ed.)*
Decadences
Morality and Aesthetics in British Literature
ISBN 3-89821-573-3

3 *Daniel M. Shea*
James Joyce and the Mythology of Modernism
ISBN 3-89821-574-1

4 *Paul Fox and Koray Melikoğlu (eds.)*
Formal Investigations
Aesthetic Style in Late-Victorian and Edwardian Detective Fiction
ISBN 978-3-89821-593-0

5 *David Ellis*
Writing Home
Black Writing in Britain Since the War
ISBN 978-3-89821-591-6

6 *Wei H. Kao*
The Formation of an Irish Literary Canon in the Mid-Twentieth Century
ISBN 978-3-89821-545-9

7 *Bianca Del Villano*
Ghostly Alterities
Spectrality and Contemporary Literatures in English
2nd, revised editon
ISBN 978-3-89821-714-9

8 *Melanie Ann Hanson*
Decapitation and Disgorgement
The Female Body's Text in Early Modern English Drama and Poetry
ISBN 978-3-89821-605-5

9 *Shafquat Towheed (ed.)*
New Readings in the Literature of British India, c.1780-1947
ISBN 978-3-89821-673-9

10 *Paola Baseotto*
"Disdeining life, desiring leaue to die"
Spenser and the Psychology of Despair
ISBN 978-3-89821-567-1

11 *Annie Gagiano*
Dealing with Evils
Essays on Writing from Africa
ISBN 978-3-89821-867-2

12 *Thomas F. Halloran*
James Joyce: Developing Irish Identity
A Study of the Development of Postcolonial Irish Identity in the Novels of James Joyce
ISBN 978-3-89821-571-8

13 *Pablo Armellino*
Ob-scene Spaces in Australian Narrative
An Account of the Socio-topographic Construction of Space in Australian Literature
ISBN 978-3-89821-873-3

14 *Lance Weldy*
Seeking a Felicitous Space on the Frontier
The Progression of the Modern American Woman in O. E. Rölvaag, Laura Ingalls Wilder, and Willa Cather
ISBN 978-3-89821-535-0

FORTHCOMING (MANUSCRIPT WORKING TITLES)

Kevin Cole
Levity's Rainbow
Menippean Poetics in Swift, Fielding, and Sterne
ISBN 3-89821-654-3

Zeynep Z. Atayurt
'Excessive' Embodiment in Contemporary Women's Writing
ISBN 978-3-89821-978-5

Rana Tekcan
The Biographer and The Subject: A Study on Biographical Distance
ISBN 978-3-89821-995-2

Fatma Tuba Terci
Postmodern Goddesses in Contemporary Chicana Feminist Novel
Peel my Love Like an Onion, Caramelo, or, Puro Cuento: A Novel and Face of an Angel
ISBN 978-3-8382-0023-1

Paola Brusasco
Writing Within / Without / About Sri Lanka
The construction of conflictual identities through cartography, history and language in selected works by M. Ondaatje and C. Muller
ISBN 978-3-8382-0075-0

Series Subscription

Please enter my subscription to the series **Studies in English Literatures**, ISSN 1614-4651, as follows:

❒ complete series OR ❒ English-language titles
❒ German-language titles

starting with
❒ volume # 1
❒ volume # ___
❒ please also include the following volumes: #___, ___, ___, ___, ___, ___, ___
❒ the next volume being published
❒ please also include the following volumes: #___, ___, ___, ___, ___, ___, ___

❒ 1 copy per volume OR ❒ ___ copies per volume

Subscription within Germany:

You will receive every title on 1st publication at the regular bookseller's price incl. s & h and VAT.

Payment:
❒ Please bill me for every volume.
❒ Lastschriftverfahren: Ich/wir ermächtige(n) Sie hiermit widerruflich, den Rechnungsbetrag je Band von meinem/unserem folgendem Konto einzuziehen.

Kontoinhaber: ____________________ Kreditinstitut: ____________________
Kontonummer: ____________________ Bankleitzahl: ____________________

International Subscription:

Payment (incl. s & h and VAT) in advance for
❒ 10 volumes/copies (€ 319.80) ❒ 20 volumes/copies (€ 599.80)
❒ 40 volumes/copies (€ 1,099.80)
Please send my books to:

NAME ____________________ DEPARTMENT ____________________
ADDRESS ____
POST/ZIP CODE ____________________ COUNTRY ____________________
TELEPHONE ____________________ EMAIL ____________________

date/signature ____

Please fax to: **0511 / 262 2201 (+49 511 262 2201)**
or mail to: ***ibidem***-Verlag, Julius-Leber-Weg 11, D-30457 Hannover, Germany
or send an e-mail: ibidem@ibidem-verlag.de

***ibidem*-Verlag**
Melchiorstr. 15
D-70439 Stuttgart
info@ibidem-verlag.de

www.ibidem-verlag.de
www.ibidem.eu
www.edition-noema.de
www.autorenbetreuung.de

Zeitfracht Medien GmbH
Ferdinand-Jühlke-Straße 7
99095 Erfurt, Deutschland
produktsicherheit@kolibri360.de